Classic & Warbird Recognition

Peter R. March

First published 1996

ISBN 0 7110 2423 5

Published by Ian Allan Publishing
An imprint of Ian Allan Publishing, Terminal House, Station Approach, Shepperton, Surrey TW17 8AS.
Printed by Ian Allan Printing Ltd, Coombelands House, Coombelands Lane, Addlestone, Surrey KT15 1HY.

Abbreviations

ehp	equivalent horsepower
ft	feet
hp	horsepower
in	inches
kN	kilonewtons
kW	kilowatts
lb	pounds (weight)
m	metres
st	static thrust

CONTENTS

Acknowledgements

The author would like to thank Robby Robinson, and Brian and Jean Strickland for their assistance with the preparation and checking of the text.

All of the copyright illustrations in abc Classic and Warbird Recognition are from the PRM Aviation Photo Library, as credited: Andrew March (APM), Daniel March (DJM), Peter R. March (PRM) and Brian Strickland (BSS).

Front cover: Boeing B17G Flying Fortress and Lockheed PV-2 Harpoon. *PRM*

Rear cover: Supermarine Spitfire. *PRM*

INTRODUCTION

This first edition of *abc Classic and Warbird Recognition* has been produced in series with *abc Civil Airliner Recognition, abc Combat Aircraft Recognition* and *abc Light Aircraft Recognition.* The title 'Classic and Warbird' covers the many vintage, veteran, retired warplanes and classic aircraft that have been preserved in flying condition, most of which have not been included in the three previous titles.

The book provides a recognition guide to the diverse types of mainly civilian-operated classic and warbird aircraft that appear at airshows and historic events around the world. They range from the unique Blenheim and Airacobra to the abundant Mustangs, Spitfires, Tiger Moths and a host of light vintage aircraft. Space does not permit the inclusion of some of the modern military and classic types, or the more common homebuilt replicas that appear at airshows. In general only those types that are currently represented by potentially flyable aircraft — examples actively being prepared to fly — like the Vulcan and Lightning, have been included.

The aircraft are presented in the established 'Recognition Series' format, under the individual heading of the design company and/or principal manufacturer followed by the aircraft's general descriptor. Standard headings are used to provide data on the aircraft's powerplant, dimensions and speed. Where known, the first flight date of the prototype is shown, followed by a broad outline of the production, including an indication of the number of the type produced. A new heading 'Survivors' gives general details of the number of the type known to be still in existence and in potentially flyable condition. The key recognition features of the aircraft are then described. Photographs are shown with each type of aircraft to help with recognition.

After the detailed presentations further brief descriptions are provided covering a selection of types that merit inclusion for the specific reasons stated, such as the Fairey Flycatcher and Vickers Vimy replicas. To assist in locating specific aircraft by name and/or manufacturer, a comprehensive index and cross-reference has also been provided.

Classic and Warbird Collections

Many of the **UK**'s active classic and warbird aircraft can be seen at air displays during the summer.

Bournemouth International Airport, Dorset — **Jet Heritage Foundation** flies a single-seat Hawker Hunter F4, the only display-flying Meteor NF11 in the world, a de Havilland Vampire T-55. Also, the **Royal Jordanian Air Force Historic Flight** (Hunter T7/F58, Vampire T55/FB6). The **Source Classic Jet Flight** is the world's largest non-government owned military jet formation team with four de Havilland Vampires and four ex-Swiss Air Force Venom FB50s.

Coventry, Warwickshire — **Air Atlantique,** operates Europe's biggest fleet of big piston-engined classic airliners — Douglas DC-3s and DC-6s — plus smaller aircraft under the **Air Antique** title.

Cranfield, Bedfordshire — **Kennet Aviation** flies two HS Gnat T1s, a Piston Provost, the only airworthy Jet Provost T1 and a Jet Provost T5A

Duxford, Cambridgeshire, houses the Imperial War Museum's large collection of (non-flying) aircraft. The IWM also operates the RAF's Messerschmitt Bf 109G and Shuttleworth's Sea Hurricane. Also based at Duxford, **The Aircraft Restoration Company** operates among others the world's only airworthy Bristol Blenheim and Wessex Aviation & Transport's Westland Lysander. **The Fighter Collection** has the only flying examples in Europe of the P-38J Lightning, F8F Bearcat, P-47D Thunderbolt, F6F Hellcat, P-63 Kingcobra, Spitfire XIV and the F7F Tigercat, plus many other active aircraft. **The Old Flying Machine Company's** fleet includes an F-86A Sabre, T-33 Silver Star, MiG-15, MiG-17, P-51D Mustang, Spitfire IX, Spitfire XI, Messerschmitt Bf109, Iraqi Fury, Corsair, T-6 Harvard and Yak-50. **Plane Sailing Air Displays** has a PBY-5A Catalina. **B-17 Preservation Ltd** flies the famous Boeing B-17 Sally B

Exeter, Devon — The **Lightning Flying Club** has a Lightning T5 and two F6s, while the **Classic Jets Aircraft Company** flies Hawker Hunters.

Isle of Wight (Sandown) Airport — the **Island Aeroplane Co** has a fleet of ex-German classic aircraft.

Middle Wallop, Hampshire — **Army Air Corps Historic Flight,** comprises a Skeeter, Sioux, Scout, Auster AOP9 and Beaver. The Museum of Army Flying also houses several airworthy vintage aircraft.

RAF Coningsby, Lincolnshire — **RAF Battle of Britain Memorial Flight**, comprises four Spitfires, a Hurricane, Lancaster and a Dakota.

Rendcomb, Gloucestershire — **Aerosuperbatics**, a fleet of Boeing Stearman biplanes in the colours of the Crunchie Flying Circus, plus de Havilland biplanes and an Antonov An-2.

RNAS Yeovilton, Somerset — as well as the extensive Fleet Air Arm Museum, the **RN Historic Flight** has two Swordfish, a Firefly and a Sea Hawk.

Old Warden, Bedfordshire — The **Shuttleworth Collection** has 34 flyable historic aircraft from the early Bleriot, and Boxkite through to World War 2 aircraft

Swanton Morley, Norfolk — a large number of Stearman biplanes operated by **Eastern Stearman**.

Wycombe Air Park, Buckinghamshire — **The Blue Max Movie Aircraft Collection** flies aircraft from the Bleriot through to the Spitfire.

Mainland Europe

Significantly fewer active classic and warbird aircraft. The two main exceptions are:-

The Netherlands — The **Duke of Brabant Air Force** operates a B-25J Mitchell and has a light aircraft section. A P-51D Mustang and a Beech YC-43 Staggerwing are also flown. The **Dutch Dakota Association** has a fleet of big piston airliners — two Douglas DC-3s and a DC-4.

Denmark, Norway and Sweden — The **Scandinavian Historic Flight** has a comprehensive collection of airworthy aircraft and is the only civilian organisation in Europe authorised to fly Mach 2.0 high-performance jets. Aircraft operated include a 1909 Thulin (Bleriot XI), 1919 Tummelisa, Boeing PT-17 Stearman, North American AT-6G Harvard, North American P-51D Mustang, Douglas A-26B Invader, De Havilland Vampire FB6, Hawker Hunter F58 and Saab J-35 Draken.

North America

In the USA and Canada many hundreds of classic and warbird aircraft fly regularly. Owners often belong to operators' associations and groups such as Warbirds of America and there are two major umbrella organisations — the Confederate Air Force and Planes of Fame.

The **Confederate Air Force** and its American Airpower Heritage Flying Museum is a world famous collection of flyable World War 2 aircraft.Its headquarters is at Midland Texas, but most of the CAF's 140 aircraft are located at other airfields. The fleet ranges from a B-24 Liberator and B-29 Superfortress to rare aircraft like the P-39 Airacobra and Japanese Zero. Texas also has a number of other active collections, including the **Cavanaugh Flight Museum** at Addison Airport, Dallas, the **Coleman Warbird Museum** at Coleman, and the **Lone Star Flight Museum** at Galveston.

The **Planes of Fame** collection at Chino, California has a number of very rare aircraft amongst its potentially airworthy machines, most notably the Northrop 'Flying Wing' and the Bell YP-59A Airacomet.

Formed in 1973, the **Canadian Warplane Heritage**, at Hamilton, Ontario, has many flyable aircraft, including a Lancaster, Hurricane, Firefly and Anson.

Above: A privately owned and operated Aeronca C3. **APM**

Aeronca C3/100

Single-engined high-wing ultra-light monoplane
Data for Aeronca 100
Powerplant: One 30.0kW (40hp) JAP J-99 engine
Span: 10.97m (36ft 0in)
Length: 6.10m (20ft 0in)
Maximum speed: 152.9km/h (95mph)
First aircraft flown: 1934
History: The Aeronautical Corporation of America designed and produced the ultra-light two-seater at Cincinnati, and Light Aircraft Ltd of Hanworth, Middlesex built a number powered by a British-built JAP J-99. This Aeronca E113C engine had dual ignition and was manufactured under licence by J. A. Prestwich Ltd (JAP).
Survivors: Seven Aeronca C3/100s remain in the UK of which four are currently flyable. There are a number of survivors in the USA.
Recognition: A 'bathtub'-shaped fuselage with a stub nose and wings of equal chord with rounded tips. Distinctive tall mast above centre of wing that supports an array of bracing wires. Large fin and rudder, which looks out of proportion. Braced tailplane set on top of fuselage. Undercarriage main wheels alongside forward fuselage.

Aeronca 0-58/ L-3/L-16

Above: Privately owned Aeronca 0-58B Defender restored to military configuration. **PRM**

Single-engined high-wing light aircraft
Powerplant: One 48.9kW (65hp) Continental 0-170-3 piston engine
Span: 10.7m (35ft 0in)
Length: 6.4m (21ft 0in)
Maximum speed: 140km/h (87mph)
First aircraft flown: 1941
History: The US Army held trials of light aircraft produced by Piper, Taylorcraft and Aeronca, for observation and liaison duties in 1941. The Aeronca Model 65TC Defender, initially designated 0-58, was put into production for observation duties, later becoming the L-3 with increased window area for liaison flying. A total of 1,390 examples of the 0-58/L-3 were built during World War 2. Postwar the US Army

purchased the L-16, a military development of the civil Model 7BC Champion, powered by a 67kW (90hp) Continental 0-205-1 engine.

Survivors: Five 0-58/L-3s and two L-16s are currently airworthy in the UK as well as numerous examples of the Chief, Super Chief and Champion.

Recognition: High-wing monoplane. Wing has parallel chord and rounded tips and is supported by V-wing struts from the lower fuselage. Humped-back appearance with two relatively deep glazed side windows (four on L-16). Fixed tailwheel undercarriage, with cross bracing between wheels. Rounded fin and rudder. Tandem seating.

Antonov An-2

Single-engined general purpose biplane

Powerplant: One 746kW (1,000hp) PZL Kalisz ASz-621R or Shevetsov ASR 621R nine-cylinder radial engine

Span: Upper 18.18m (59ft 7.75in); Lower 14.24m (46ft 8.5in)

Length: 12.74m (49ft 9.5in)

Maximum speed: 258km/h (160mph)

First aircraft flown: 31 August 1947 (First Polish version 23 October 1960)

Above: *Antonov An-2T based at Sandown with the Island Aeroplane Company.* ***PRM***

Below:Utterly Butterly*, an Antonov An-2T operated by* Aerosuperbatics.

History: Designed to a specification of the Ministry of Agriculture and Forestry in the USSR, the An-2 first entered production in 1948. Over 5,000 examples were built in the Soviet Union. Limited production continues in China and by PZL Mielec in Poland (with over 12,000 built). An-2 has been exported to many countries in three basic versions: the An-2P as a 12-seat passenger version, An-2R as an agricultural version with tanks for dry or liquid chemicals, and An-2T as a general purpose transport version.

Survivors: Several An-2s are currently operated in the UK including G-BTCU, painted in Soviet AF markings and based at Henstridge; HA-MEP owned by Vic Norman at Rendcomb and displayed as *Utterly Butterly*; and OM-UIN that is leased during the summer by Avia Special.

Recognition: Large single-engined biplane of unequal span with single bay. Fuselage of circular section with 'birdcage' cockpit canopy set ahead of upper wing. Circular side windows and large door midway along port side. Fixed tailwheel undercarriage with split axle. Single radial engine with large single exhaust on starboard side. Four-blade propeller.

Left: *1946-built Auster J-1N Alpha.* ***PRM***

Auster Autocrat/Alpha/AOP

Single-engined high-wing light aircraft
Data for J-1 Autocrat

Powerplant: One 74.5kW (100hp) Blackburn Cirrus Minor 2 four-cylinder in-line air-cooled inverted engine
Span: 10.97m (36ft 0in) ***Length:*** 7.13m (23ft 5in) ***Maximum speed:*** 161km/h (120mph)
First aircraft flown: 1945 (Auster 5 J-1)

History: Auster Aircraft Ltd was a successor to Taylorcraft Aeroplanes (England) Ltd which was formed in 1939 to manufacture a cabin monoplane under licence from Taylorcraft Aircraft Corporation of America. The company became Auster Aircraft Ltd on 7 March 1946. The Taylorcraft Auster 5 series J-Autocrat was designed during the last year of World War 2, adapting the Blackburn Cirrus Minor 2 to the military Auster AOP5 airframe for civil sales. Over 400 Autocrats were built by Auster Aircraft at Rearsby. A number were later re-engined with the DH Gipsy Major 1, fitted with a larger fin and rudder and designated J-1N Alpha.

Survivors: Examples of the following types in addition to the Autocrat/Alpha remain active in the UK: Auster Mks 3, 4, 5, 6, 7, AOP9, AOP11, Aiglet, Aiglet Tr, Alpine, Arrow, Autocar, Workmaster, D4, D6, J-4 and several Taylorcraft and Beagle variants.

Recognition: Most of the series are externally similar. Engine and tail shapes differ slightly. All have V-strut wing bracing and parallel chord wings. Fixed taildragger undercarriage. The J-1B Aiglet had wider fuselage and reduced wingspan; J-5B Autocar four seat J-1 with high-back rear fuselage; J-5F Aiglet Trainer — two-seat trainer version with clipped wings; Auster AOP — 108kW (145hp) Gipsy Major VIII (also Beagle Terrier); Auster AOP9 — 134kW (180hp) Cirrus Bombardier 203 engine, single wing struts.

Avro 504K

Single-engined biplane trainer

Powerplant: One 82.7kW (110hp) Le Rhône rotary engine ***Span:*** 10.97m (36ft 0in)
Length: 8.97m (29ft 5in) ***Maximum speed:*** 152.9km/h (95mph) ***First aircraft flown:*** 1917

History: The first Avro 504A was flown in 1913 and versions A-H were produced in the early part of World War 1. The front universal engine mounting was introduced in 1917 to accept larger engines, thus becoming the 504K. More than 8,000 Avro 504s were built, the majority being used as basic pilot trainers. Some were used by the RFC for bombing and reconnaissance. Postwar the 504K equipped all of the RAF Flying Training Schools until 1924, when it was replaced by the Lynx-engined 504N. At the end of 1935 the Air Ministry refused to renew C of As for rotary-engined aircraft — and the heyday of the 504K was over.

Survivors: There are two airworthy Avro 504Ks in the UK: an original 504N (H5199/G-ADEV) rebuilt by the Shuttleworth Trust at Old Warden in 1955 and a privately-owned replica (G-ECKE) built in 1994. It has a Warner Scarab engine and is painted in Royal Flying Corps colour scheme as D8781. Four other examples are held by UK museums and at least eight 504s are preserved around the world, only one being airworthy.

Above: *Avro 504K Replica, built in 1994, flies with the Great War Display Team.* ***PRM***

Recognition: Staggered two-bay biplane of equal span. Two open cockpits, in tandem. Slim rear fuselage to a point with small elliptical fin. External control wires to square-tipped tailplane, which has pronounced centre rear cut-out. Most distinctive feature is an ash skid, anchored to fuselage by steel V-struts, ahead of main wheels and axle. Engine is usually cowled on upper half.

Avro Tutor

Single-engined two-seat elementary biplane trainer

Powerplant: One 160.3kW (215hp) Armstrong Siddeley Lynx IVc seven-cylinder radial piston engine

Span: 10.36m (34ft 0in)

Length: 8.07m (26ft 6in)

Maximum speed: 196.7km/h (122mph)

First aircraft flown: December 1929

Above: *The Shuttleworth Collection has operated this Avro Tutor since 1959.* ***PRM***

History: The original Avro Trainer of 1929 was designed as a replacement for the Avro 504K and featured a 115.5kW (155hp) Armstrong Siddeley Mongoose IIIA radial engine. The Tutor was chosen to succeed the 504N in the RAF's Flying Training Schools after three years of comparative trials with various elementary trainers. More than 390 Tutors were built for the RAF, 14 Sea Tutors, and a number were sold to Denmark, Greece and Poland. Some were built under licence in South Africa. The Tutor became standard equipment at the RAF's CFS, all Flying Training Schools and with the University Air Squadrons until 1939. A total of 795 Tutors were constructed.

Survivors: Sole surviving Tutor in the UK is K3215/G-AHSA with the Shuttleworth Collection at Old Warden. It was built in 1932 and used by No 1 FTS. Stored during the war, it was restored in 1947 and has been flown by Shuttleworth since 1959.

Recognition: Heavily staggered, equal span, two-bay biplane. Townend ring over engine cylinders. Square wing tips. Tandem open cockpits. Oblong braced tailplane with V cut-out for rudder. Fixed long travel braced undercarriage. Fixed tail skid.

Avro Anson XIX

Twin-engined low-wing monoplane

Powerplant: Two 313.2kW (420hp) Armstrong Siddeley Cheetah 15 seven-cylinder radial engines

Span: 17.52m (57ft 6in)

Length: 12.88m (42ft 3in)

Maximum speed: 302km/h (188mph)

First aircraft flown: 24 March 1935 (Anson 1)

History: The Anson was the RAF's first monoplane and aircraft with a retractable undercarriage to enter service. It competed with the de Havilland Dragon Rapide to win an order for a coastal reconnaissance aircraft. Production commenced in December 1935 with deliveries to No 48 Squadron Manston in spring 1936. The early examples featured a hand-operated dorsal turret. For 3½ years they were the backbone of Coastal Command. Following the arrival of the Lockheed Hudson, the Anson was gradually withdrawn from front-line service and relegated to communications and training duties. Production ran for 17 years and 11,020 Ansons were built; the last (a T21) was delivered to the RAF on 27 May 1952.

Survivors: There are two airworthy Ansons surviving in the UK amongst a number held by museums and collections. Restoration of Anson 19 Srs 2 G-AHKX has been completed at Woodford after a lengthy rebuild; while WD413/G-BFIR is expected to be flying again in 1996 after overhaul.

Recognition: Low-wing monoplane with straight leading edge and rounded tips. Pronounced rear wing fillet. Main wheel undercarriage does not fully retract, leaving lower part of tyre exposed. Distinctive diamond tailplane that is low-set. Fixed tailwheel. Large curved tail fin. Anson 1 featured continuous cabin glazing whereas the Mks11 to 22 had individual side windows. Pronounced forward-facing horn balance to rudder.

Above: *This newly restored Avro 19 Srs 2 Anson is based at Woodford.* **PRM**

Below: *Avro Anson T21 restored in a RAF Transport Command colour scheme.* **PRM**

Above: *Owned and operated by the Canadian Warplane Heritage Avro Lancaster B10 is the second airworthy example of the type.* **PRM**

Avro Lancaster B1

Four-engined heavy bomber

Powerplant: Four 962.4kW (1,280hp) Rolls-Royce Merlin 24 piston engines

Span: 31.09m (102ft 0in) ***Length:*** 21.13m (69ft 4in)

Maximum speed: 461.8 km/h (287mph) ***First aircraft flown:*** 9 January 1941

History: Developed from the twin-engined Avro 679 Manchester, and originally known as the Manchester III, BT308 was a converted Manchester with four Merlin engines in lieu of the troublesome Rolls-Royce Vulture engines. The first production Lancaster I (L7527), first flew on 31 October 1941. Production concluded in 1946 after 7,374 had been built. The first operational mission was flown on 3 March 1942 by No 44 Squadron from RAF Waddington. Lancasters formed the mainstay of Bomber Command operating with 56 squadrons. They flew a total of 156,000 wartime missions. Postwar the Lancaster operated mainly in the maritime reconnaissance role until 1956.

Survivors: Only the RAF Battle of Britain Memorial Flight's Lancaster B1 PA474 is airworthy in the UK; a second airworthy aircraft (ex RCAF B10MR – FM159/KB726/C-GVRA) is operated by the Canadian Warplane Heritage from Hamilton, Ontario. There are more than 20 Lancasters surviving in museums and collections around the world.

Recognition: Mid-wing four-engined monoplane. Four Merlin engines are low-slung on slightly swept wing leading edge and are staggered in plan form. Twin elliptical tail fins/rudders at extremity of low-set tailplane. Glazed nose, dorsal and rear turrets. Glazed rounded bomb-aimer's nose panel. Forward cockpit under transparent canopy with small astrodome at rear. Retractable main undercarriage but fixed tailwheel.

Right: *Avro Lancaster B1 flown by the RAF Battle of Britain Memorial Flight at RAF Coningsby.* **PRM**

Above: *Avro Shackleton AEW2 (WL790) is being restored to fly again in the USA.* ***PRM***

Avro Shackleton MR2

Four-engined long-range maritime patrol aircraft
Data for: Shackleton AEW2
Powerplant: Four 1,842.1kW (2,450hp) Rolls-Royce Griffon 57A piston engines
Span: 36.58m (120ft 0in)
Length: 26.59m (87ft 3in)
Maximum speed: 474.7km/h (295mph)

First aircraft flown: 9 March 1949 (MR1); 30 September 1971 (AEW2)
History: Originally planned as an anti-submarine Lincoln 3, the Shackleton was designed to meet a 1946 Coastal Command requirement. It used the Lincoln mainplane and undercarriage, together with many Tudor assemblies and was fitted with Griffon engines driving six-blade contra-rotating propellers. The first production MR1 (VP254) was first flown on 24 October 1950 and 77 were built up to July 1952. The MR2 with a longer nose and retractable dustbin radar followed in 1952 (69 built) and the redesigned MR3 with a tricycle undercarriage and wing-tip tanks first flew on 2 September 1955 (34 built, plus eight for the South African Air Force). Twelve AEW2s were converted from MR2s in the early 1970s.
Survivors: None are currently airworthy in the UK but Air Atlantique has two Shackleton AEW2s, one of which is being prepared to fly again in the USA.
Recognition: Four-engined mid-wing monoplane. Slightly swept leading edge to the wing with rounded tips. Low-slung Griffon engines with contra-rotating propellers. Extended nacelles to the rear of the inboard engines. Deep fuselage, featuring squat cockpit and extending to a pointed glass tail cone at rear. Pointed nose with pronounced dorsal glazed canopy. Large twin oval fins/rudders. High-set tailplane. Retractable mainwheels and twin tailwheels. AEW2 version features large and distinctive ventral radome.

Avro Vulcan B2

Long-range, four-jet, heavy bomber
Powerplant: Four 89.06kN (20,000lb st) Bristol Siddeley Olympus 301 turbojets
Span: 38.83m (111ft 00in)
Length: 30.45m (99ft 11in)
Maximum speed: 1037.9km/h (645mph)
First aircraft flown: 30 August 1952 (B1); 31 August 1957 (B2)

Right: *Avro Vulcan B2 XH558 is preserved in flying condition at Bruntingthorpe.* ***PRM***

History: The world's first delta wing heavy bomber, the Vulcan B1 entered operational service in the RAF with No 83 Squadron on 11 July 1957. With a larger wing and more powerful engines, the Vulcan B2 was able to carry a bigger bomb load further, higher and faster. As a nuclear bomber, it was equipped to carry the supersonic Blue Steel cruise type air-to-surface missile. During the Falklands conflict of 1982 the Vulcan dropped bombs in anger when the airfield at Port Stanley was attacked on several occasions. The last Vulcans, converted as refuelling tankers, were withdrawn in 1984 — but one was kept airworthy for airshow appearances until 1992. Production of the Vulcan totalled 134.
Survivors: A number of Vulcans survive in museums and collections in Britain and North America. Three aircraft in the UK have been kept in near airworthy condition (XH558 at Bruntingthorpe, XL426 at Southend and XM655 at Wellesbourne Mountford). All three have their engines run regularly and are taxied.
Recognition: Large delta wing with no tailplane. Swept fin and rudder. Cranked leading edge on the B2. Elevons in four sections.

BAC (English Electric) Lightning T5/F6

Single-seat, twin turbojet, all-weather interceptor fighter
Data for Lightning F6
Powerplant: Two 58.78kN (13,200lb st; 16,300lb st with reheat) Rolls-Royce RA34R Avon 310 series engines, installed one above the other
Span: 10.61m (34ft 10in)
Length: 16.84m (55ft 3in)
Maximum speed: Mach 2.1 (2,419.4km/h/1,500mph)
First aircraft flown: 4 August 1954 (P1A prototype); 16 June 1965 (F6[Interim]) 3 November 1959 (F1)

Above: *BAC (English Electric) Lightning F6 XS904 is owned by the Lightning Preservation Group at Bruntingthorpe.* ***PRM***

History: The RAF's first single-seat fighter able to exceed the speed of sound in level flight and the first fighter designed as an integrated weapons system. It had an operational ceiling (60,000ft/18,288m) far in excess of any previous RAF fighter. The Lightning F3 became Fighter Command's principal air defence fighter in 1964. The T5 was a two-seat trainer version of the F3. The F6 (first flown 17 April 1964) was a longer range development of the F3. It was the last of the RAF's long line of classic single-seat fighters, remaining in squadron service over 20 years. Two squadrons (Nos 5 & 11) remained on interceptor duties with Strike Command at RAF Binbrook until the late 1980s, when they were finally replaced by Tornado F3s. A small number continued to fly with BAe at Warton as trials and target aircraft.
Survivors: Lightning T5 rebuilt at Plymouth and another restored at Cranfield to flying condition. The three former BAe F6s have been kept airworthy at Exeter and Binbrook by the Lightning Flying Club. The CAA had not permitted any of them to fly, as at the end of 1995.
Recognition: Sharply swept (60°) wings with parallel chord. Low-set, swept tailplane. Large, round nose air intake, with a conical nose cone. Small cockpit well ahead of leading edge of wing. Deep fuselage with two engines and jet pipes one above the other. Tall pointed swept fin. Large curved belly fuel tank under fuselage.

Left: *This Beech D-17S Staggerwing is kept in flying condition at Popham.* ***PRM***

Beech 17 Staggerwing

Single-engined four-seat cabin biplane

Powerplant: One 335.3kW (450hp) Wright R-975 nine-cylinder radial engine
Span: 9.76m (32ft 0in)
Length: 7.98m (26ft 2in)
Cruising speed: 312km/h (195mph)
First aircraft flown: 4 November 1932
History: In 1932 Walter H. Beech founded the Beech Aircraft Co and the first aircraft produced was the Model 17 biplane. It entered production in 1934. The basic design was improved in 1936 and the following year had full-span flaps fitted on the lower wings and ailerons on the upper wings. During World War 2, 425 were produced for the US Forces and some were issued to the RAF for communications duties. Twenty were produced postwar with Wasp Junior engines and other refinements. Staggerwing production ceased in 1948 after a total of 781 Model 17s had been completed.
Survivors: Four Staggerwings are airworthy in the UK and Eire, including NC18028 and G-BRVE based at North Weald. The first USAAC YC-43 Traveler is based in the Netherlands with the Duke of Brabant Air Force.
Recognition: Equal-span single-bay biplane with back stagger. Upper wing attached direct to the top of the fuselage with one 'I'-type steel interplane strut on either side of the fuselage. Wings of equal chord with rounded tips. Enclosed cabin with door on port side. Inward retracting undercarriage. Retractable tailwheel. Close cowling to engine and two-bladed propeller. Near vertical leading edge to the fin with curved trailing edge. Raked windscreen.

Beech T-34 Mentor

Single-engined two-seat primary trainer
Data for T-34B Mentor
Powerplant: One 168kW (225hp) Continental 0-470-13 flat-six piston engine
Span: 10.01m (32ft 10in) ***Length:*** 7.87m (25ft 10in)
Maximum speed: 304.8km/h (189mph) ***First aircraft flown:*** 2 December 1948
History: The Beech 45 was inexpensively developed from the Bonanza as a tandem two-seat primary trainer and in March 1953 the USAF selected it as the new primary trainer with the designation T-34A Mentor, over 450 being built. A year later the US Navy also adopted the Mentor (designated T-34B) and 423 were delivered. In 1973 Beech received a USN contract to

Above: *Beech T-34A in RCAF markings and a US Navy-painted T-34B Mentor, flying in Florida.* ***PRM***

upgrade T-34Bs with a 298kW (400shp) PT6A-25 turboprop. A total of 300 T-34Cs (some being new-build) were ordered, deliveries beginning in November 1977.

Survivors: A large number of former USAF and US Navy T-34A/Bs are operated by private owners in North America.

Recognition: Low-wing monoplane. Tapered wings with wing root fillet at base of forward leading edge. Deep oval fuselage. Large domed glazed dual-cockpit canopy. Upright leading edge to tail fin with sloping trailing edge and small dorsal extension. Tapered tailplane. Retractable tricycle undercarriage.

Beech 18 Expeditor

Twin-engined light transport aircraft

Powerplant: Two 335kW (450hp) Pratt & Whitney Wasp Junior R-985-AN-14B radial engines

Span: 14.5m (47ft 8in)

Length: 10.4m (34ft 3in)

Maximum speed: 371km/h (230mph)

First aircraft flown: 15 January 1937

Above: *Beech C-45 Expeditor II, finished in a World War 2 South East Asia colour scheme, is based at North Weald.* ***DJM***

History: The Model 18 was built as a light eight-seat commercial transport, 5,204 military examples being produced in World War 2, in addition to prewar civil and postwar military and civil models. It served with the USAAF as the UC-45A transport and communications aircraft, AT-7 navigation trainer and AT-11 Kansan bombing and gunnery trainer; the US Navy version was the JRB-1/2 and it was named the Expeditor in RAF, RN and RCAF service. The Model 18 was improved throughout its production and five models appeared with Wright, Jacobs and Pratt & Whitney engines. The postwar Super 18 incorporated a number of refinements including an optional tricycle undercarriage. Developments by Volpar and others have produced turbo-prop, stretched and executive versions.

Survivors: In 1996 there were just two airworthy Beech 18s in the UK. There are a number of others across Europe and many in North America covering all of the wartime variants and later developments.

Recognition: Low-wing monoplane. Tapering outer wing sections. Oval tapering fuselage with twin fins and rudders. Pilot's compartment in nose, with side-by-side seating. Normally three large oblong windows on each side of the fuselage in passenger compartment.
Passenger door on port side.

Bell P-39 Airacobra

Single-engined, single-seat fighter

Powerplant: One 867.7kW (1,150hp) Allison V-1710-35 12-cylinder Vee liquid-cooled engine

Span: 10.37m (34ft 0in)

Length: 9.2m (30ft 2in)

Maximum speed: 606km/h (385mph)

First aircraft flown: XP-39 6 April 1938; YP-39 13 September 1940

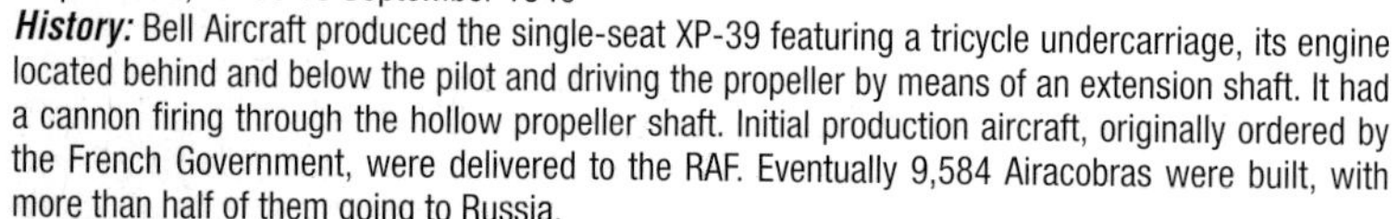

Above: *This Bell P-39 Airacobra is preserved by the Confederate Air Force in flying condition at San Marcos, Texas.* ***PRM***

History: Bell Aircraft produced the single-seat XP-39 featuring a tricycle undercarriage, its engine located behind and below the pilot and driving the propeller by means of an extension shaft. It had a cannon firing through the hollow propeller shaft. Initial production aircraft, originally ordered by the French Government, were delivered to the RAF. Eventually 9,584 Airacobras were built, with more than half of them going to Russia.

Survivors: There are over 40 surviving Airacobras, but only one airworthy example with the Confederate Air Force in Texas. There are a further three on rebuild, including one destined for The Fighter Collection at Duxford. Most of the survivors were recovered in the 1980s in Papua New Guinea.

Recognition: Low-wing cantilever monoplane. Wings of equal tapering chord with rounded tips. Mid-fuselage engine installation with exhaust stubs behind cockpit. Curved cockpit over leading edge of wing, with entry door on port side. Oval fuselage. Raised dorsal scoop behind cockpit for air-intake to engine. Rounded fin and rudder. Curved fuselage underside. Tailplane set level with top of rear fuselage. Fully retractable tricycle undercarriage.

Bell P-63 Kingcobra

Single-engined, single-seat fighter-bomber

Powerplant: One 996.2kW (1,325hp) Allison V-1710-93 liquid-cooled engine

Span: 11.69m (38ft 4in)

Length:9.96m (32ft 9in)

Maximum speed: 660km/h (410mph)

First aircraft flown: 7 December 1942

History: The P-63 Kingcobra was developed from the P-39, with bulk of the production of 3,303 going to the USSR as a ground attack aircraft under Lend-Lease arrangements. It was not used operationally by the USAF, but served with Advanced Training Units. Over 300 flew with the Free French Air Force. A heavier and bigger aircraft, it featured a laminar flow wing. Equipped with a hydraulically-driven supercharger the P-63 had an increased ceiling and high altitude performance.

Survivors: There are 15 known P-63 survivors — five of which are maintained in flying condition and a further five are being restored to fly. One airworthy Kingcobra is operated by The Fighter Collection at Duxford and another by the Confederate Air Force in Texas.

Recognition: Low-wing cantilever monoplane. Wings of equal tapering chord with rounded tips.

Mid-fuselage engine installation with exhaust stubs behind cockpit. Curved cockpit, over leading edge of the wing and port entry door. Oval fuselage and pronounced, raised, dorsal scoop behind cockpit for engine air-intake. Angular fin and rudder. Tailplane set level with top of rear fuselage. Fully retractable tricycle under-carriage with long oleo to nosewheel.

Above: *This Bell P-63A Kingcobra is operated by Bob Pond's Planes of Fame in the USA.* ***PRM***

Bleriot Type XI

Single-engined, single-seat monoplane
Powerplant: One 18.8kW (25hp) Anzani radial engine
Span: 7.77m (25ft 6in)
Length: 8.00m (26ft 3in)
Maximum speed: 72.41km/h (45mph)
First aircraft flown: 23 January 1909
History: The Bleriot Type XI was the most significant European aircraft in the pre-World War 1 period. Originally flown with a 30hp REP engine, it was modified to take a more efficient 25hp Anzani air-cooled, semi-radial, three-cylinder engine. It made the first powered flight across the English Channel on 25 July 1909, flown by Louis Bleriot in 37min. The Bleriot was later used by both the Naval and Military wings of the Royal Flying Corps up to 1915. Later aircraft were powered by a more powerful Gnôme radial engine.

Above: *Bleriot Type XI flown by the Jean-Baptiste Salis Association at La Ferté-Alais, France.* ***APM***

Survivors: Two examples are airworthy in the UK: G-AANG, a 1910 original, is with the Shuttleworth Trust at Old Warden and G-BPVE, a replica built in the USA in 1967, is operated by Bianchi Aviation Film Services at Wycombe Air Park. Other Bleriot replicas are flown in Europe and North America.
Recognition: Tubular-framed fuselage, partly covered by fabric, tapering to small tail fin. Very low-set tailplane. Open cockpit. Engine close to the leading edge of wing, which has pronounced convex curvature with wire bracing throughout. Large 'bicycle type' main wheels.

Boeing B-17G Flying Fortress

__Above:__ Based at Duxford, Boeing B-17G Flying Fortress Sally B *is owned and operated by B-17 Preservation. It is one of two airworthy examples in Europe.* ***DJM***

Four-engined heavy bomber

Powerplant: Four 894.8kW (1,200hp) Wright Cyclone R-1820-97 radial engines

Span: 37.47m (103ft 9in)

Length: 22.66m (74ft 4in)

Maximum speed: 463km/h (287mph)

First aircraft flown: 28 July 1935

History: In May 1934 the US Army Air Corps issued a specification for a multi-engine, anti-shipping bomber to defend the nation against enemy fleets. In 1938 the USAAC placed an order for 39 production B-17Bs. These were equipped with turbocharged engines that provided a higher maximum speed and increased service ceiling. The B-17E was armed with 12 machine guns and named the Flying Fortress. Most extensively built was the B-17G that had a chin turret below the nose. A total of 12,731 B-17s were produced. After the war a number were used for aerial photography, training, drone-direction, search and rescue, fire-bombing and meteorological research flying.

Survivors: There are over 50 surviving B-17s, of which 12 are currently airworthy, including one in Britain (*Sally B* based at Duxford) and another in France.

Recognition: Four-engined bomber with wings of equal taper and rounded tips. Very large, rounded fin and rudder, with rounded top and dorsal fillet forward of leading edge. Angular tailplane set half-way up the fuselage at rear. Chin nose turret. 'Cheek' mounted guns on either side of nose, twin-gun turret on top of fuselage aft of the pilot's cockpit, 'ball' ventral turret and gun position in rear, and on both sides of fuselage, midway between wings and tail. Small pilot's compartment seating two, side-by-side. Retractable tailwheel, but main wheels do not fully retract into inner-engine nacelles.

Boeing-Stearman Kaydet

Above: Boeing-Stearman PT-13A Kaydet is based at Swanton Morley in Norfolk. ***DJM***

Below: Boeing-Stearman PT-17, one of four operated by the Crunchie Flying Circus. ***APM***

Single-engined biplane trainer
Powerplant: One 164.0kW (220hp) Continental R-670-5 radial piston engine
Span: 9.80m (32ft 2in)
Length: 7.54m (24ft 10in)
Maximum cruising speed: 171km/h (106mph) ***First aircraft flown:*** 1934
History: In 1934 Lloyd Stearman developed a two-seat biplane trainer of very clean lines and as a private venture. Later in the same year the company became a subsidiary of the Boeing Company and the trainer was developed (as the Model 70), winning an Army Primary Trainer competition. Known as the Boeing-Stearman Kaydet, over 8,000 were built for the US Army and Navy. The N2S-2 for the US Navy had a 209kW (280hp) Lycoming R-680-8 and PT-13B for the USAAC the R-680-11 engine. The PT-17 was similar, with the Continental engine. Post-World War 2 surplus PTs were acquired by civil operators, many being converted for use as agricultural dusters or sprayers.
Survivors: There are over 1,000 PT-17s and variants surviving, with 40 active in the UK. Powerplants vary from 220hp to 360hp. The popular *Crunchie Flying Circus* operates four 'big-engined' Stearmen for its wing-walking display team.
Recognition: Large seven-cylinder radial engine with exposed cylinders. Biplane of equal length, parallel chord and rounded tips. Cantilever main undercarriage in taildragger configuration, usually without wheel spats. Twin open cockpits. Pointed fin with curved trailing edge to rudder. Braced tapered tailplane.

Above: Currently the only airworthy example, Bristol Blenheim IVT, is the second of the type to be restored by the Aircraft Restoration Co. ***PRM***

Bristol Blenheim

Twin-engined light bomber
Powerplant: Two 686kW (920hp) Bristol Mercury XV radial air-cooled engines
Span: 17.17m (56ft 4in)
Length: 13.00m (42ft 7in)
Maximum speed: 460km/h (285mph)
First aircraft flown: 12 April 1935 (Blenheim I)
History: The Bristol Aeroplane Company was asked by Lord Rothermere to build an executive transport able to carry a pilot plus six passengers at 240mph. The resulting Type 142 was the first British stressed-skin monoplane with a retractable undercarriage. Its speed was greater than contemporary RAF fighters. As a result the Blenheim I bomber was developed using a new fuselage with mid-wing and a bomb bay below it. To provide a navigator/bomb-aimer station ahead of the pilot the nose was lengthened by 3ft, thus becoming the Blenheim IV. A total of 4,431 Blenheim I & IVs were produced (including the Bolingbroke in Canada).
Survivors: Over 40 Blenheims/Bolingbrokes have survived, with one currently flyable in the UK (the Aircraft Restoration Company at Duxford) and two more on rebuild to fly in North America.
Recognition: Monoplane with mid-set, tapered wings with rounded tips. The MkI had a short glazed nose whereas the MkIV had a long asymmetric nose. Both versions had a dorsal turret. The IV F featured a fighter gun pack under the nose. Angular fin on rudder. Tailplane set midway on rear fuselage with a straight leading edge and rounded tips. Main wheels do not fully retract into engine nacelle. Fixed tailwheel.

Bücker Bü 131B Jungmann

Light, two-seat, biplane trainer
Powerplant: One 74.5kW (100hp) Hirth HM 504 in-line air-cooled engine
Span: 7.39m (24ft 3in)
Length: 6.60m (21ft 8in)
Maximum speed: 185km/h (115mph)
First aircraft flown: 27 April 1934
History: The Jungmann primary training biplane was designed by the Bücker Flugzeugbau GmbH in 1933 and was built in quantity before World War 2 for both Luftwaffe elementary training units and private owners. It was subsequently built under licence in Switzerland and postwar by Construcciones Aeronauticas S A (CASA) for the Spanish Air Force as the EE-3. At one time it was used as a trainer in 21 countries and was also licence-built in Hungary and Czechoslovakia.
Survivors: Many remain airworthy, particularly across Europe. The Spanish Air Force sold its fleet to private owners, with more than a dozen now flying in the UK from a total of 32 flyable.
Recognition: Single-bay biplane with interchangeable upper and lower wings that have 11° sweepback and ailerons fitted to all four. Two open cockpits in tandem. Long main landing gear, with pronounced forward stagger, and axles hinged to pyramidal bracing under the fuselage.

Above: *CASA 1.131E Jungmann, an ex-Spanish Air Force example, restored in the UK.* ***PRM***

Right: *This view of a CASA 1.131E Jungmann shows its swept-back wings.* ***PRM***

Above: *The Cessna 120 has a single side window and does not have landing flaps.* **PRM**

Cessna 120/140

Single-engined, two-seat, cabin monoplane
Data for Cessna 140
Powerplant: One 63.4kW (85hp) Continental C85-12F flat-four engine
Span:10.0m (32ft 10in)
Length: 6.40m (20ft 11.75in)
Maximum speed: 193km/h (120mph)
First aircraft flown: 28 June 1945
History: After producing over 6,000 military aircraft during World War 2, Cessna had a manufacturing organisation geared to large-scale production. A two-seat, all-metal light aircraft, the Cessna 120, was launched and 2,171 subsequently produced between 1946 and 1949. The Model 140 was similar to the 120 but was fitted with flaps, had a slightly larger engine, a starter, generator and battery. A total of 4,907 were built by 1949.
Survivors: A large number of Cessna 120/140s are still flying in North America and more than 40 in the UK, where it is a popular vintage taildragger.
Recognition: Single-engined high-wing monoplane. Two seats side-by-side. V-bracing to wings from top of undercarriage legs. Taildragger configuration undercarriage. Rounded fin and rudder. Low-set tapered tailplane. 140 has flaps, extra side windows and the distinctive spring steel undercarriage, and the Cessna 140A has single wing support struts.

Consolidated Vultee PBY-5A Catalina

Above: *Consolidated PBY-5A Catalina, operated by Plane Sailing at Duxford.* **DJM**

Twin-engined, long-range, maritime patrol flying boat/amphibian
Powerplant: Two 895kW (1,200hp) Pratt & Whitney R-1830-92 Twin Wasp radial engines
Span: 31.72m (104ft 0in)
Length: 19.5m (63ft 11in)
Maximum speed: 314km/h (196mph)
First aircraft flown: 21 March 1935
History: Consolidated battled with Douglas in 1933 to supply the US Navy with its first cantilever monoplane flying boat. Its features included two Twin Wasps mounted close together on a wide clean wing and retractable stabilising floats at the wing tips. The PBY-5A was an amphibian (with retractable land undercarriage). Many were delivered to RAF Coastal Command and made a significant contribution to the anti-submarine offensive. Apart from its primary role as a patrol bomber, the Catalina was used as a torpedo-carrier, as a night bomber, as a convoy protection and anti-submarine weapon, for long-range reconnaissance and air-sea rescue duties. Many

Catalinas have continued in service as transport aircraft and for fire-bombing until very recently.

Survivors: Currently there are five European-based, airworthy Catalinas (including Plane Sailing's aircraft based at Duxford), with more under restoration amongst a large number in North and South America.

Recognition: Semi-cantilever high-wing monoplane. The wing centre-section is supported above the hull by a streamline superstructure and braced by two pairs of parallel streamline struts to the sides of the hull. Two-step semi-circular topped hull. Retractable wing tip floats. Lower part of the fin is integral with the hull. Tailplane is set midway on fin. Small glazed cockpit seating two side-by-side. Two large transparent gun-blisters on the sides of the hull aft of the wings.

Above: *The Dutch Historic Flight's Consolidated PBY-5A Catalina.* ***DJM***

Consolidated Vultee B-24 Liberator

Four-engined, long-range, heavy bomber

Powerplant: Four 895kW (1,200hp) Pratt & Whitney R-1830-43 radial engines

Span: 33.5m (110ft 0in)

Length: 20.47m (67ft 2in)

Maximum speed: 467km/h (290mph)

First aircraft flown: 29 December 1939

History: The Liberator was built in larger numbers than any other American aircraft in history, in more versions for more purposes, and served on every front in World War 2 and with 15 Allied nations. Though conceived five years after the B-17 Flying Fortress it was not a great improvement, except on range. All the flying controls were electrically powered. The B-24C introduced power-driven dorsal and tail turrets. Ten 12.7mm (1/2in) machine guns were carried and up to 3,629kg (8,000lb) of bombs were carried internally. It was also built as a long-range transport. Total B-24 production was 19,203.

Survivors: Nineteen Liberators survive of which just two are airworthy, both based in the USA: one with the Confederate Air Force in Texas, the other operated by the Collings Foundation in Florida.

Recognition: High-wing monoplane featuring a Davis wing of high aspect ratio and constant taper from roots to tips. Four radial engines with short nacelles. Main undercarriage legs retracted outwards into wings. Retractable nosewheel. Large Fowler flaps between ailerons and fuselage. Two large rounded fins and rudders. Later models had power-driven turret in nose with bombardier's prone position below.

Above: *Consolidated LB-30A Liberator based with the Confederate Air Force at Midland, Texas.* ***PRM***

Curtiss P-40 Warhawk/Kittyhawk

Single-engined, single-seat fighter

Powerplant: One 782kW (1,040hp) Allison V-1710-33 12-cylinder liquid-cooled engine

Span: 11.38m (37ft 4in)

Length: 9.68m (31ft 9in)

Maximum speed: 576km/h(357mph)

First aircraft flown: 14 October 1938

History: The P-40 was a development of the P-36, substituting an in-line engine for the radial. The P-40A was supplied to the RAF as the Tomahawk II. The majority of USAAF examples were allocated to the Pacific area. The RAF purchased 560 P-40Ds as the Kittyhawk I and had a Rolls-Royce Merlin 28. P-40F was the Kittyhawk II fitted with a 1,240hp Packard V-1650-1 (Rolls-Royce Merlin) 28 engine. The P-40N Kittyhawk III, the most produced Warhawk variant, had a 1,200hp Allison engine and was built in 1943-44. P-40s of later variants served with USAAF units in the Middle East and Pacific areas, but the greater proportion went under Lend-Lease to Allied nations, mainly Britain, Russia, China, South Africa, Australia and New Zealand. Total production was 15,000.

Survivors: Over 70 P-40s are known to exist of which 20 are in flying condition and a similar number on rebuild. There are two examples currently based in Europe.

Recognition: Low-wing cantilever monoplane. Enclosed pilot's cockpit over trailing edge of wing. Chin-mounted engine radiator. Tapering wings with rounded tips. Tailplane set on top of rear fuselage. Rounded fin and rudder. Retractable main wheels which retract aft and up. Fully retractable tailwheel. Three-blade propeller. Most airworthy P-40s have a passenger seat behind the pilot.

Above: *Privately owned in the USA this Curtiss P-40N Warhawk is painted in 'Flying Tigers' colour scheme.* ***PRM***

Left: *Curtiss P-40M Kittyhawk III now flown from La Ferté Alais in France.* ***PRM***

Above: The DH60G Moth features a non-inverted engine, with the exhaust on top of the fuselage. PRM

De Havilland DH60G Gipsy Moth

Single-engined sport biplane
Powerplant: One 89.5kW (120hp) de Havilland Gipsy II engine
Span: 9.14m (30ft 0in)
Length: 7.29m (23ft 11in)
Maximum speed: 165km/h (102mph)
First aircraft flown: 1927
History: In 1927 the de Havilland Company started manufacturing the Gipsy engine. In a derated form it was fitted to the DH60 Moth, for club and private use, so becoming the Gipsy Moth. The Gipsy Moth will always be associated with Amy Johnson, who made the epic flight to Australia in May 1930 with G-AAAH *Jason*. The wooden Gipsy Moth continued until 1934, with British production totalling 595. The metal fuselage Gipsy Moth (DH60M) was introduced for overseas customers in 1928. With the advent of the superior metal fuselage production of Gipsy Moths quickly ended.
Survivors: There are some two dozen DH60 Moths of all varieties surviving in the UK, with more overseas. The oldest, a Cirrus-engined Moth (G-EBLV), was first flown in 1925 and remains active with the Shuttleworth Collection at Old Warden.
Recognition: Equal-span, single-bay biplane, its unstaggered wings having straight leading and trailing edges with swept tips. The centre-section fuel tank is carried above the fuselage on N-struts. Fuselage of rectangular wooden structure is covered with fabric. The DH60M can be identified by a number of prominent stringers under the fabric. Typical de Havilland shape tail empennage. The engine is not inverted and it has a long exhaust pipe with the manifold on top of the engine.

Above: *Recently restored ex-Spanish DH60G Moth.* ***PRM***

De Havilland Tiger Moth

Single-engined biplane trainer
Powerplant: One 96.9kW (130hp) de Havilland Gipsy Major engine
Span: 8.94m (29ft 4in)
Length: 7.29m (23ft 11in)
Maximum speed: 176km/h (109mph)
First aircraft flown: 26 October 1931
History: Developed from the DH60 Gipsy Moth, the Tiger Moth was powered by an inverted Gipsy III engine. The DH82A also differed from the Gipsy Moth in having swept back and staggered wings. The centre-section struts were moved forwards. By 1939 over 1,000 had been built, mainly for the RAF and civilian flying schools. During the war over 4,200 Tiger Moths were built at Cowley and Hatfield, with nearly 3,000 more in Canada, New Zealand and Australia. By the early 1950s the RAF had replaced it with the Chipmunk, and many examples were sold to the civilian owners in the UK and overseas.
Survivors: A large number of Tiger Moths remain flyable around the world, particularly in the countries where they were manufactured. There are nearly 200 currently registered in the UK, although they are not all in airworthy condition.
Recognition: Equal-span single-bay biplane. Wings are staggered and swept back. Ailerons on lower wings only. Centre section, incorporating the fuel tank, is carried above the fuselage, on N-struts. Fuselage of rectangular steel-tube structure, covered with fabric. Tandem open cockpits with dual controls. Split type landing gear with rubber-in-compression springing. Typical DH rear empennage.

Above: *One of many ex-RAF de Havilland DH82A Tiger Moths flown in the UK by members of the DH Moth Club.* ***PRM***

De Havilland DH83A Fox Moth

Single-engined cabin biplane
Powerplant: One 96.9kW (130hp) de Havilland Gipsy Major I piston engine
Span: 9.40m (30ft 10.5in)
Length: 7.85m (25ft 9in)
Maximum speed:173km/h (107mph) ***First aircraft flown:*** March 1932
History: The Fox Moth was built as a short-range, light transport development of the Tiger Moth. It featured the tail unit, wings, undercarriage and engine mounting married to a new, larger fuselage which accommodated a forward cabin for up to four passengers and a rear, open, pilot's cockpit. The DH83 was initially powered by the 120hp (89.4kW) DH Gipsy III, but later machines (DH83A) have the 130hp (96.9kW) Gipsy Major. Ninety-eight were produced by the parent company at Stag Lane, 48 of these being registered in Britain and the remainder sold abroad. In 1945 de Havilland Canada produced a further 50 DH83Cs with an enclosed pilot's cockpit.
Survivors: A quartet of Fox Moths remain airworthy in the UK, including the most recently restored example G-ACEJ based at Rendcomb, Glos.
Recognition: Equal-span single-bay biplane. The centre-section fuel tank is carried above the passenger cabin fuselage on N-struts. Wings are staggered and slightly swept back. Ailerons on lower wings only. Fuselage of rectangular steel-tube structure, covered with fabric. Open cockpit for pilot and passenger cabin for four passengers, with two windows on each side of fuselage, situated between the wings. Typical DH fin and rudder. Split type main undercarriage.

Left: *De Havilland DH83 Fox Moth — a 1933 British-built version has an open pilot's cockpit.* ***PRM***

De Havilland DH87B Hornet Moth

Below: *De Havilland DH87B Hornet Moth first registered in 1936 has the later square-tipped wings.* ***DJM***

Single-engined cabin biplane

Powerplant: One 96.9kW (130hp) de Havilland Gipsy Major I piston engine

Span: 9.48m (31ft 11in)

Length: 7.63m (24ft 11.5in)

Maximum speed: 200km/h (124mph)

First aircraft flown: 9 May 1934

History: The Hornet Moth was designed as a two-seat, cabin biplane for private and club flying. The original DH87 and the initial production model, the DH87A Hornet Moth I, had wings with sharply tapered tips, but in 1936 the DH87B Hornet Moth II, with square-tipped wings of reduced span and larger area, replaced the earlier model. One hundred and sixty-five were constructed between 1935 and 1938 of which 84 were registered in Britain. Many were impressed into RAF service for communications duties during World War 2. Some Hornet Moths were fitted with floats.

Survivors: Some 16 DH87B Hornet Moths remain on the UK civil register, of which the majority are currently airworthy.

Recognition: Equal-span single-bay biplane with square tips. Wings are slightly staggered and swept. Ailerons on lower wings only. Glazed cockpit for two with side-by-side seating directly under the upper wing. Typical DH tail fin and rudder, and tailplane. Main undercarriage at mid-fuselage, with two bracing struts.

De Havilland DH89A Dragon Rapide

Twin-engined, six/eight-seat, passenger biplane

Powerplant: Two 149.1kW (200hp) de Havilland Gipsy-Six air-cooled in-line engines

Span: 14.6m (48ft 0in)

Length: 10.52m (34ft 6in)

Maximum speed: 253km/h (157mph)

First aircraft flown: April 1934

History: An improved version of the DH84 Dragon or a scaled-down, twin-engined DH86B, the DH89 Dragon Six as it was initially named, was designed as an eight-seat biplane for short-range commercial operators. Production of the Dragon Rapide commenced in 1935 and during World War 2 many DH89B aircraft were delivered to the RAF for use as radio and navigation trainers under the name Dominie. With the end of the war, a number of airframes laid down for the RAF were completed for commercial operators, and many ex-RAF machines were converted for civil use. A total of 697 DH89s had been completed when production ceased in 1946. Postwar the mini-airliner re-entered commercial service and remained in limited numbers until the mid-1960s.

Survivors: There are eight flyable Dragon Rapides from a total of 18 in the UK; there are others in Europe, Australia and New Zealand.

Recognition: Equal-span braced biplane, with noticeably tapered wings. Upper surfaces are attached directly to the top of the fuselage. Tubular drag-struts and wire bracing. Tapered ailerons on all four wings. Narrow, slab-sided fuselage. Tailplane is wire-braced to the fin. Typical de Havilland tail fin and the rudder has a horn-balance. Entire structure is of wood with fabric covering. Trousered undercarriage legs under each engine nacelle. Enclosed cabin for pilot in extreme nose. Glazed cabin windows back to port entry door half-way along fuselage.

Above: *A de Havilland DH89A Rapide, in 1935 Prince of Wales colour scheme, is privately owned at Henstridge.* ***PRM***

Left: *Based at Rendcomb, Glos, this de Havilland DH89A Rapide was built in 1936.* ***PRM***

De Havilland DH98 Mosquito TIII/B35

Twin-engined fighter-bomber
Data for Mosquito B35
Powerplant: Two 1,260kW (1,690hp) Rolls-Royce Merlin 113/114 piston engines
Span: 16.51m (54ft 2in)
Length: 12.34m (40ft 6in)
Maximum speed: 669km/h (415mph)
First aircraft flown: 25 November 1940
History: The Mosquito was the fastest aircraft in service with the RAF from its entry into service in September 1941 to the arrival of a new generation of fighters in 1944. It remained the RAF's fastest bomber until the appearance of the pure jet Canberra. The Mosquito was produced in 40 different versions in Britain, Canada and Australia with a total of 7,781 being built. This wooden-construction monoplane, utilising two Merlin engines, relied on high speed for defence. The last Mosquito, an NF38, was completed on 15 November 1950. The final RAF operational flight by a front-line squadron Mosquito was flown by PR34 RG314 of No 81 Squadron in Malaya, on 15 December 1955.
Survivors: There are more than 30 surviving Mosquitos, most of which are located in Britain. There are only two currently airworthy — one in the UK (BAe Hawarden) and the other in Florida (Kermit Weeks). Four more Mosquitos are being restored to fly.
Recognition: Mid-wing monoplane with slightly swept wing leading edges and sharply tapered trailing edges. Centre position of the one-piece wing carries the engine mountings and radiators. Oval-section, all-wood fuselage. Elliptical tailplane, set to rear of tail fin. Side-by-side seating in small cockpit. Slim curved fin and rudder.

Above: *The only airworthy example in the UK, BAe's Chester-based de Havilland Mosquito T III.* ***PRM***

Right: *This de Havilland Mosquito B35 (RS712) is owned and based in Florida.* ***PRM***

Above: *Operated by Source Classic Jet Flight at Bournemouth, this de Havilland Vampire FB6 is painted to represent the first Royal Navy Vampire to make a carrier deck landing.* ***PRM***

De Havilland DH100 Vampire FB6/T11/T55

Single-jet-engined, single-seat fighter/two-seat night fighter/dual-control trainer
Data for DH Vampire FB6
Powerplant: One 14.91kN (3,350lb st) de Havilland Goblin 3 turbojet
Span: 11.58m (38ft 0in)
Length: 9.37m (30ft 9in)
Maximum speed: 884km/h (548mph)
First aircraft flown: 20 September 1943
History: The DH100 was designed to make best use of the new turbojet. It had a short central nacelle built of wood, housing the pressurised cockpit ahead of the engine, with wing-root inlets and a short jet pipe. The tail was carried on two booms, with the tailplane above the jet efflux. Initially known as the Spider Crab, it was the first Allied aircraft to exceed 500mph (806km/h). The second prototype (LZ551) became the world's first jet aircraft to fly on to and from an aircraft carrier on 3 December 1945. Although too late to see action in World War 2, the Vampire equipped a number of RAF and RAuxAF squadrons and overseas air arms. The DH113 Vampire NF10 was a two-seat night fighter development and the DH115 Vampire T11/T22 was a successful two-seat trainer with the RAF and RN.
Survivors: There are over 150 Vampires surviving in the UK, mainland Europe and the USA, including a small number of single-seat Vampire FB6s. With the retirement of Vampires from the Swiss AF and sale to private owners a number have been kept in flying condition. The biggest single collection of airworthy Vampires is operated by the Source Classic Jet Flight at Bournemouth Airport.
Recognition: Mid-wing monoplane with slightly swept wing leading edges and rounded tips. Twin booms with twin fins and rudders and a high-set rectangular tailplane between the fins. Central circular nacelle, with a conical nose, housing the cockpit at the front with a small bubble canopy and jet engine behind, with a short jet pipe to the rear. Air inlets in the wing roots. Main undercarriage retracts sideways into wing wheel-wells. Nosewheel retracts rearwards into nacelle pod. Twin-seat versions have a wider fuselage which has side-by-side seating.

Above: *De Havilland DH104 Dove 6, owned by the Royal Jordanian Air Force Historic Flight and based in the UK.* ***PRM***

De Havilland DH104 Dove/Devon/Sea Devon

Twin-engined, light executive transport

Powerplant: Two 283.3kW (380hp) de Havilland Gipsy Queen 70 Mk2 engines

Span: 17.37m (57ft 0in)

Length: 11.98m (39ft 4in)

Maximum speed: 338km/h (210mph)

First aircraft flown: 25 September 1945

History: The Dove was designed as a replacement for the Dragon Rapide and the prototype G-AGPJ was first flown at Hatfield in September 1945. After some early setbacks it was ordered by many overseas customers. At home the RAF adopted it for communications duties as the Devon C1, and the Royal Navy as the Sea Devon. Many improvements and modifications were incorporated during the 540 production run of the Dove. The engines later fitted included the 400hp (298kW) Gipsy Queen 70/Mk3 for the executive Mk8, the final version to be produced. The Devon was also supplied to the Indian, New Zealand, South African and Swedish Air Forces.

Survivors: Less than one-third of the 36 surviving Doves/Devons remain flyable in the UK, most of these being retired former RAE, RAF and RN aircraft.

Recognition: Low-wing monoplane with slim tapered wings and slender engine nacelles protruding forward of the leading edges. Main undercarriage retracts outwards, into the wings, behind the nacelles. Retractable nosewheel mounted at fuselage extremity. Small domed-glazed cockpit canopy. Tapered tailplane mounted low at rear of fuselage, behind the fin. Large dorsal fillet to leading edge of tail fin. Four oblong passenger windows on each side of fuselage. Entry door, with glazed panel, on port side of fuselage.

Above: *A privately owned de Havilland DH104 Dove 6 based at North Weald.* ***PRM***

Above: *An ex-Swiss Air Force de Havilland Venom FB50, is owned/operated by Source Classic Jet Flight at Bournemouth.* ***PRM***

De Havilland DH112 Venom FB50

Single-jet-engined day fighter-bomber/two-seat night and all-weather fighter

Powerplant: One 21.6kN (4,850lb st) de Havilland Ghost 103 centrifugal turbojet
Span: 12.7m (41ft 8in) inc wing-tip tanks
Length: 9.7m (31ft 10in)
Maximum speed: 1,030km/h (640mph)
First aircraft flown: 2 September 1949

History: Successor to the Vampire, the DH112 was designed to specification 15/49 with the more powerful Ghost engine. This resulted in extensive airframe changes including a new wing with very slight sweep. It had a new main landing gear and longer-span tailplane. Some 523 FB1/4s were delivered to the RAF. Later versions had an ejector seat, powered ailerons and redesigned vertical tail surfaces. Many Venoms were exported. The two-seat radar-equipped night fighter version (NF2/3) entered service in 1952. The Sea Venom FAW20/21 went to the FAA in 1953 and the FAW22 had Firestreak guided missiles and a larger Ghost 105 engine. The Aquilon was a redesigned version made by SNCASE in France (of which 114 were produced) for the Aéronavale, powered by a Fiat-built Ghost turbojet. The Venom FB50 was built by FFW in Switzerland.

Survivors: Eight former Swiss Air Force Venom FB50s are currently airworthy in the UK, four being operated by the Source Classic Jet Flight at Bournemouth. A number of flyable Venoms are in the hands of private owners in Europe and North America.

Recognition: Mid-wing monoplane with slightly swept wings. Wing-tip tanks standard. Twin booms with twin fins and rudders and a high-set rectangular tailplane between the fins. Central circular nacelle with pointed nose cone (FB50), cockpit with small bubble canopy at the front and jet engine and pen-nib jet pipe at rear. Air inlets in wing roots. Main wheels retract outwards into wheel-wells. Nosewheel retracts into nacelle pod.

De Havilland Canada DHC1 Chipmunk

Single-engined, tandem-seat, training aircraft

Powerplant: One 108.1kW (145hp) de Havilland Gipsy Major 10 Mk2 piston engine
Span: 10.46m (34ft 4in)
Length: 7.74m (25ft 5in)
Maximum speed: 200km/h (124mph)
First aircraft flown: 22 May 1946

History: Designed by the De Havilland Company in Canada, the Chipmunk was selected to replace the Tiger Moth as standard primary trainer with the RAF and RCAF. The UK air arm received 735 Chipmunk T10s. Others served with the Royal Canadian Air Force, designated T30; most had a clear-view 'blown' cockpit canopy in place of the 'glasshouse' structure of British-built Chipmunks. The civil version was also produced as the Mk21 and for agricultural crop-spraying as the Mk23. The Chipmunk was finally retired from UK military service in spring 1996.

Survivors: Over 100 civilian-owned Chipmunks are active in the UK, and a similar number in other parts of the world.
Recognition: Single-engined, low-wing monoplane with fixed taildragger undercarriage. Low-mounted tapered wings with square tips. Sliding canopy over the tandem cockpit. Distinctive de Havilland shaped fin and rudder. Tapered tailplane at fuseLage extremity.

Above: *One of many ex-RAF Chipmunks now privately owned.* ***PRM***

Douglas A-26 Invader

Twin-engined attack bomber
Powerplant:
Two 1,491kW (2,000hp) Pratt & Whitney R-2800-27 Double Wasp radial engines
Span: 21.34m (70ft 0in)
Length:
15.24m (50ft 0in)
Maximum speed:
571km/h (355mph)
First aircraft flown:
10 July 1942

Above: *Douglas A-26B Invader operated by the Scandinavian Historic Flight is based at Oslo, Norway.* ***PRM***

History: The Invader was entirely conceived, designed, developed, produced in quantity and used in large numbers during World War 2. The A-26B featured a solid nose with six machine guns while the A-26C had a transparent bomb-aimer's nose. Nearly 2,500 A-26s were built and remained in service with the USAF until the mid-1960s and even longer with the French Air Force and in South America. The reworked A-26K was used for close support duties in Indo-China with striking success. A number of A-26s were modified by On-Mark as executive transports and others were used after release by the services for other forms of aerial work. In 1948 the B-26 Marauder was retired from service and the remaining Invaders were redesignated B-26. Over 450 were used in Korea and Vietnam.
Survivors: Nearly 190 Invaders and variants are known to exist around the world, with something like 50 in flyable condition. There is currently only one airworthy A-26 in NW Europe.
Recognition: The low-drag laminar-flow wings are shoulder mounted. Fuselage is practically square with rounded corners in cross-section. Underslung engines and nacelles protrude behind trailing edge of wing. Dihedral tailplane. Two two-gun electrically-operated turrets, one above and one below the fuselage, and both remotely controlled from a gun-sighting station aft of the wings. Tall fin and rudder, with square top, and fillet at lower leading edge. Main wheels retract into engine nacelles and nosewheel rotates through 90° to lie flat in the bottom of the fuselage.

Douglas AD-4 Skyraider

Single-engined naval torpedo and dive bomber
Powerplant: One 2,252kW (3,020hp) Wright R-3350-26WA radial engine
Span: 15.24m (50ft 0in)
Length: 11.63m (38ft 2in)
Maximum speed: 512km/h (318mph)
First aircraft flown: 18 March 1945

Above: *A Douglas AD-4NA Skyraider owned and based in Florida.* ***PRM***

History: Planned in 1944 as the first single-seat, torpedo/dive bomber, the XBT-2D competed against three rival designs. The Skyraider's versatility led to many modifications for additional missions. A total of 242 AD-1s were built, of which 35 were ECM aircraft. The AD-3 was an anti-submarine detection/strike version, while the refined AD-4 was built in the largest number (1,032). The AD-4W had a large belly radome to accommodate airborne early warning radar, 40 being supplied to the Royal Navy in 1952. More than 1,000 Skyraiders served in Vietnam where it proved to be one of the most effective combat types.
Survivors: There are more than 50 surviving Skyraiders of which about half are potentially flyable. The Fighter Collection operates an AD-4NA from Duxford.
Recognition: Low-wing monoplane, with square tips to the equal-taper, dihedralled wings. Large radial engine and deep fuselage. Small bubble canopy for single-seater — extended glazed canopy for dual-seaters. Large angular fin and rudder with curved dorsal fillet. Tailplane has swept leading edge and straight trailing edge. Retractable taildragger undercarriage.

Douglas C-47 Skytrain/DC-3 Dakota

Twin-engined, medium range, transport aircraft
Powerplant: Two 894.8kW (1,200hp) Pratt & Whitney Twin Wasp R-1830-90C radial engines
Span: 28.9m (95ft 0in)
Length: 19.6m (64ft 6in)
Maximum speed: 369km/h (229mph)
First aircraft flown: 22 December 1935
History: The C-47 was a military transport version of the commercial DC-3 airliner. It was adopted as standard transport by the Allied Air Forces during World War 2 and 10,926 had been built when production ceased. The C-47 was known as the Skytrain by the USAAF/USN, and Dakota by the RAF, RCAF and RAAF. It was built in the Soviet Union as the Li-2. During World War 2 there were numerous versions, some civil aircraft impressed into military use, some paratroopers and tugs. The vast majority were utility C-47s with a cargo floor and large double doors. The first Dakota entered RAF service in June 1942 and played a vital part in the Normandy landings and postwar in the Berlin Airlift. Douglas DC-3s and Dakotas are still used by civilian operators throughout the world.
Survivors: There are several hundred Dakotas remaining airworthy around the world. In the UK Air Atlantique at Coventry has a fleet of ten aircraft for passenger/cargo and anti-maritime pollution operations.
Recognition: Low-wing monoplane having swept outer wings, with dihedral and pointed tips. Short engine nacelles mounted close inboard. Almost circular-section fuselage with six large square windows on each side. Large entry door at rear of port side. Large tail fin and rudder with a small dorsal fillet. Main wheels partially retract into engine nacelles, tailwheel fixed. Swept leading edge, straight trailing edge to tailplane.

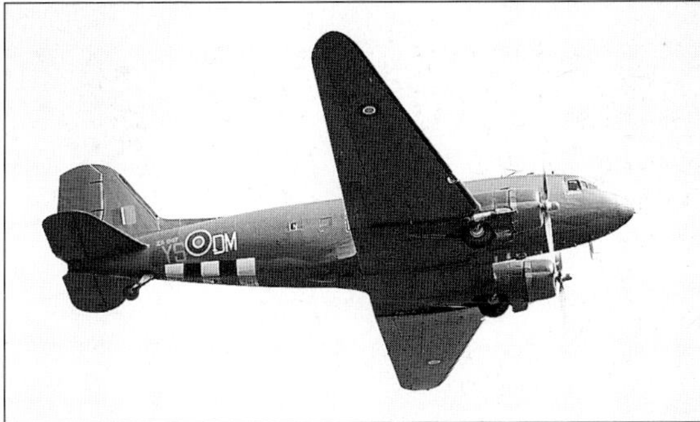

Left: *The Battle of Britain Memorial Flight at RAF Coningsby uses this Douglas Dakota C3 for crew training and communications.* ***PRM***

English Electric Canberra B6/TT18

Twin-turbojet bomber, interdictor, photo-reconnaissance and training aircraft
Data for Canberra B6
Powerplant: Two33.4kN (7,500lb st) Rolls-Royce Avon 109 single-shaft turbojets
Span: 19.5m (63ft 11.5in)
Length: 19.95m (65ft 6in)
Maximum speed: 935 km/h (580mph)
First aircraft flown: 13 May 1949
History: Designed to Specification B3/45 as a Mosquito replace-ment, the Canberra B1prototype (VN799) was followed by the B2 on 21 April 1950. The RAF received 430 of this initial production version. The Canberra B2 entered squadron service at Binbrook in May 1951 and remained in front-line service with Bomber Command for the next ten years. Subsequent variants developed included the PR3, PR7 and PR9 for photo-reconnaissance; the B6 and the B15/B16 bomber conversions; and the T4, T11, T17, T19 and T22, many of which were modified from earlier marks, all for specialised training duties. Only a handful of PR7/9s remain in RAF service.
Survivors: Apart from the RAF aircraft operated by No 39 (1 PRU) Squadron at RAF Marham, there are three civilian-owned Canberras kept airworthy in the UK, based at Bruntingthorpe and North Weald, and three in the USA.
Recognition: The Canberra PR9 has a long pencil fuselage with a distinctive cockpit offset to the port side, while the B6/TT18 survivors have the traditional wide canopy. Deep-chord wings taper towards the tips with engines mounted in the wings and projecting forward. Angular fin and rudder, square-tipped with the dihedralled tailplane set on top of the fuselage cone. Main wheels retract inwards into the wing.

Above: *English Electric Canberra TT18 is kept flying by Mitchell Aircraft.* ***PRM***

Fairchild PT-23/ PT-26 Cornell

Single-engined, primary trainer monoplane

Powerplant: One 149kW (200hp) Ranger L-440-7 six-cylinder in-line inverted piston engine

Span: 10.97m (36ft 0in)

Length: 8.51m (27ft 11.4in)

Maximum speed: 203km/h (126mph)

First aircraft flown: March 1939

History: The tandem two-seat (normally with open cockpits) Fairchild M-62 was produced in three versions as a primary training monoplane for the USAAF and others. The PT-19 (built by Fairchild and Aeronca) was powered by a 130.4kW (175hp) Ranger L-440-1 inverted engine. The PT-23 (built by Howard and St Louis Aircraft) was identical in construction to the PT-19B but powered by a 164kW (220hp) Continental R-670 radial engine. The PT-26 was powered by the 149kW (200hp) Ranger L-440-7 engine. This version had a sliding cockpit canopy. As well as serving with the USAAF, it was adopted by the Canadian Government as the standard primary trainer for the Commonwealth Air Training Plan and built by Fleet Aircraft in Canada. It was used by the RAF as the Cornell. Production ceased in 1944 by which time some 8,000 had been produced.

Survivors: There are many examples of all variants surviving in North America, although there are only four potentially airworthy in the UK.

Recognition: Low-wing monoplane, the wings having equal taper with rounded tips. Fixed taildragger undercarriage. Fuselage of steel-tube framework with fabric covering. Pointed tail fin/rudder. Tailplane set high on rear fuselage. Tandem cockpits, open on PT-19 and PT-23 or under a long sliding canopy (PT-26).

Top: *A Fairchild PT-23 operated by the PT Flight in the UK.* ***PRM***

Above: *This Texas-based Fairchild PT-26 is painted as an RAF Cornell with an enclosed cockpit.* ***PRM***

Fairchild Argus

Single-engined light transport aircraft

Powerplant: One 149kW (200hp) Ranger L-440-7 six-cylinder in-line inverted air cooled engine

Span: 11.7m (36ft 4in) ***Length:*** 7.24m (23ft 10.5in)

Maximum speed: 198km/h (124mph)

First aircraft flown: 1933 (three-seater); 1937 (four-seater)

History: The original three-seat Fairchild Model 24 was replaced in production by a four-seat version, the Model 24J in 1937. A further-improved light military utility transport, the Forwarder was produced in 1942 for the Royal Air Force, under the name Argus I. It was subsequently adopted by the US Army under the designation C-61, and fitted with a 145hp (108kW) Warner R-500-1 Super-Scarab radial engine. This was followed by the C-61A with the more powerful R-500-7 engine. In 1944 the UC-61K Argus III was fitted with the Ranger in-line engine. Postwar a number of Warner-engined 24Ws were converted for civilian use in the UK.

Survivors: There are six flyable Ranger-engined Argus IIIs operating in the UK, some being converted from Super-Scarab powered Argus Is, their original engines being used to power replica World War 1 aircraft.

Recognition: High-wing, braced monoplane, the wings tapering in plan and section where they join the fuselage. Friese-type ailerons. Rectangular steel-tube structure covered with fabric. Divided type landing gear — each unit consists of an oleo leg, the top attached to the front wing bracing strut, with the bottom end hinged to the bottom fuselage. Enclosed cabin, seating four in two pairs.Sloping windshield and side windows. Entry doors on each side of the fuselage.

Top: *A privately owned Fairchild Argus III painted in USAAF markings, operates from Speke.* ***PRM***

Above: *This F24R-46A Argus has the civilian spatted and faired undercarriage.* ***PRM***

Fairey Firefly AS5

Single-engined naval fighter and anti-submarine aircraft
Powerplant: One1,674kW (2,245hp) Rolls-Royce Griffon 74 piston engine
Span: 12.55m (41ft 2in)
Length: 11.56m (37ft11in)
Maximum speed: 618km/h (386mph)
First aircraft flown: 22 December 1941

History: Designed as a Fleet reconnaissance aircraft to Specification N5/40, the Firefly was developed from the Fulmar. It was initially powered by a 1,730hp (1,290kW) Rolls-Royce Griffon in place of the Merlin. The first production Firefly I Z1830 was delivered to RNAS Yeovilton on 4 March 1943. The main wartime version was the Mk1, widely used from the end of 1943 in all theatres. Fairey and General Aircraft built 429 F1s, 376 FR1s with ASH radar and then 37 NF2 night fighters. The more powerful MkIII followed, from which the FR4, with two-stage Griffon engine and wing-root radiators, was developed. The FR4s were subsequently succeeded by the FR5, AS6 and AS7s. In 1956 the Firefly gave way to the Avenger and Gannet with front-line RN squadrons.

Survivors: There are two-dozen Fireflies known to exist, of which only two — the RN Historic Flight's AS5 (WB271) and one in Canada are currently airworthy. Four more Fireflies are under restoration to fly in the USA and Australia.

Recognition: Low-wing monoplane with folding elliptical wings (with square tips) housing four cannon and with the trailing edge provided with Youngman flaps for use at low speeds. Oval-section fuselage with the cockpit over the wing leading edge, with the observer behind the wing. Wing-root radiators on later models — chin radiator on early versions. Inward-retracting main wheels and retractable tailwheel.

Top: *Fairey Firefly AS5 operated by the RN Historic Flight at RNAS Yeovilton.* ***PRM***

Left: *The RN Historic Flight's Firefly shows its large landing flaps.* ***PRM***

Above: *Fairey Swordfish II LS326 operated for many years by the RN Historic Flight at RNAS Yeovilton.* ***PRM***

Fairey Swordfish II

Single-engined torpedo carrier/ spotter reconnaissance biplane

Data for Swordfish II

Powerplant: One 559kW (750hp) Bristol Pegasus 30 radial engine

Span: 13.87m (45ft 6in)

Length: 10.87m (35ft 8in)

Maximum speed: 224km/h (139mph)

First aircraft flown: 17 April 1934

Above: *Fairey Swordfish IV, a Canadian-built example, restored by BAe and now also flies with the RN Historic Flight.* ***PRM***

History: The Swordfish or 'Stringbag' as it was known has a significant place in the history of naval aviation. It outlasted the aircraft that was intended to replace it and served successfully throughout World War 2. The prototype K4190 was derived from the TSR1 flown the year previously. From 1940 all production and development was handled by Blackburn, which built 1,699 of the 2,391 delivered — the last aircraft (NS204) left the lines on 18 August 1944. The highlight of the Swordfish's service was the attack on the Italian naval base of Taranto on 10-11 November 1940. The last Swordfish Squadron, No 836, disbanded on 21 May 1945.

Survivors: More than 15 Swordfish survive, of which two are airworthy in the UK with the RN Historic Flight at Yeovilton, and two in North America.

Recognition: Two-bay, unequal-span, staggered wing biplane. Upper centre-section carried on pyramid structure, lower centre-section stubs braced to upper fuselage by inverted V-struts. Ailerons on all four wings. Wings fold round rear spar hinges. Fixed divided type undercarriage. Townend cowling ring over nine-cylinder radial engine. Rectangular steel-tube fuselage structure, metal covered at front and fabric at rear. Large curved fin and rudder. Braced tailplane.

Fieseler Fi 156C Storch

Top: *This Argus in-line engined Morane-Saulnier MS500 is based at the Imperial War Museum, Duxford.* ***PRM***

Above: *A radial-engined MS505 is flown by the Aircraft Restoration Company at Duxford.*

Single-engined, short take-off and landing, general purpose aircraft
Powerplant: One 179kW (240hp) Argus As410C in-line engine
Span: 14.25m (46ft 9in)
Length: 9.90m (32ft 6in)
Maximum speed: 176km/h (109mph)
First aircraft flown: 1936

History: The Storch was developed specifically for slow-speed flying and operating from restricted spaces. It was used throughout World War 2 on various military duties, the Fi 156A-1 being the first production type; the Fi 156C-1 serving as a staff transport; the Fi 156C-2 as a short-range reconnaissance aircraft; and the Fi 156D as an air ambulance. Others were used for general-purpose and army co-operation duties. It was also built by Morane-Saulnier in occupied France (MS500 series with the MS502 Criquet having a Salmson 9AB radial engine), by Benes Mraz in Czechoslovakia and Meridionali in Italy. It remained in production in France until 1948. A total of 1,549 Fi 156s were built.

Survivors: Several dozen Fi 156s and MS500 series remain in Europe, particularly France. There are four surviving in the UK, including one Fi 156.

Recognition: High-wing monoplane, with constant chord wings hinged to the upper fuselage and braced to the lower fuselage by steel-tube V-struts. Entire wing trailing edge hinged as slotted camber-changing flaps. Rectangular steel-tube fuselage covered with fabric. Entire sides and roof of cabin glazed. Side windows built out with lower panels sloping in to give good downward vision. Door on starboard side. Long split type undercarriage legs. Slender rear fuselage leading to broad fin and rudder. Braced tailplane.

Above: A black-painted Fokker Dr1 Triplane replica based at the Museum of Army Flying at Middle Wallop. **PRM**

Fokker Dr1 Triplane

Single-seat fighting scout triplane
Powerplant: One 82.02kW (110hp) Le Rhône nine-cylinder rotary engine
Span: 7.17m (23ft 7.5in)
Length: 5.77m (18ft 11in)
Maximum speed: 165km/h (103mph)
First aircraft flown: June 1917
History: The impressive combat performance of the Sopwith Triplane so startled the German Air Force that Fokker was instructed to build a similar fighter. It entered service in August 1917 and remained in production until June 1918. The JG1 'circus' of Manfred von Richthofen was the first unit to be equipped and Richthofen himself was flying his scarlet Dr1 when he was shot down on 21 April 1918.
Survivors: There are no known original Fokker Dr1s surviving but a number of replicas have been constructed, including two in the UK. Sadly, one of these was destroyed in a fatal accident in July 1995.
Recognition: Triple rectangular wings have neither a dihedral nor an arrow angle. They are staggered vertically and the spans are unequal, growing smaller from the top plane to the lowest. The upper plane alone has ailerons which project beyond the wing tips. Undercarriage has a streamlined axle, which is so deep that it forms a fourth lifting surface. Tailplane is a large triangle with rounded tips. Small, almost circular fin. Single open cockpit set level with trailing edge of centre wing. The top plane is cut away in the middle to enable the pilot to see upwards and forwards.

Above: Fokker DVII replica privately owned in the UK. **PRM**

Fokker DVII

Single-seat fighting scout
Powerplant: One 119.3kW (160hp) Mercedes DIII six-cylinder water-cooled engine
Span: 8.9m (29ft 2in)
Length: 6.95m (22ft 9.75in)
Maximum speed: 189km/h (117mph)
First aircraft flown: January 1918
History: Developed from a long line of successful German fighter aircraft, the DVII, which appeared in early 1918, had an excellent performance and caused great concern to the Allies. The first examples were sent to von Richthofen's JG1 (that was commanded by Hermann Goering after Richthofen's death) in April 1918. Over 1,000 examples had been produced by the Armistice. After World War 1 a number of DVIIs was assembled by Anthony Fokker in Holland and were used by the Dutch Air Force.
Survivors: There are seven surviving authentic Fokker DVIIs, all of which are preserved in non-flying condition. Replica flying examples have been built in Europe and North America. One German-built DVII remains active in the UK.
Recognition: The extreme depth of wing section and the absence of external bracing wires are distinctive features. Both upper and lower staggered wings are without dihedral and are in one piece, passing above and below the fuselage respectively. Slender V-struts to undercarriage. Open cockpit set over trailing edge of lower wing. Tapered rear fuselage to a rounded rudder, and a small triangular dorsal fin. Single strut-braced tailplane on top of the rear fuselage. Fixed tail skid.

Above: *Gloster Gladiator I, owned by The Shuttleworth Collection at Old Warden.* ***PRM***

Gloster Gladiator

Single-seat fighter
Powerplant: One 626kW (840hp) Bristol Mercury IX nine-cylinder radial engine
Span: 9.85m (32ft 3in)
Length: 8.38m (27ft 5in)
Maximum speed: 407km/h (253mph)
First aircraft flown: September 1934
History: The Gladiator was the RAF's last biplane fighter. It was designed by H. P. Folland as a private venture to Specification F7/30. It was ordered by the RAF and the first Gladiator I was flown in June 1936. The fighter remained in production until April 1940 by which time total production was 767 — including 480 for the RAF, 60 Sea Gladiators for the Fleet Air Arm and 216 exported. It first entered squadron service in February 1937 when No 72 Squadron was re-equipped at Tangmere. They were not to remain in the front line for long as the Hurricane and Spitfire were quickly appearing on the scene.
Survivors: There are two potentially flyable Gladiators in the UK. The Shuttleworth Collection's aircraft has been active since 1951 and a Sea Gladiator is currently being restored to fly by The Fighter Collection at Duxford.
Recognition: Single-bay biplane, with each of the four planes having small hydraulically-depressed drag flaps. Rounded wing tips. Cantilever landing gear with internally-sprung wheels. Sliding cockpit canopy set to the rear of the trailing edge of the upper wing. Large Townend cowling with individual domed covers to the nine-cylinders. Tapering rear fuselage to large rounded fin and rudder.

Above: *The Gladiator has a fixed undercarriage and a distinctive round-topped fin and rudder.* ***APM***

Above: *The only airworthy Gloster Meteor F8 has been restored by the Classic Jets Flying Museum.* ***PRM***

Gloster Meteor F8/NFII

Twin turbojet fighter/night fighter
Data for Meteor F8
Powerplant: Two 16 kN (3,600lb st) Rolls-Royce Derwent 8 turbojets
Span: 11.33m (37ft 2in)
Length: 13.58m (44ft 7in)
Maximum speed: 951.6km/h (590mph)
First aircraft flown: 5 March 1943
History: The Meteor was designed to meet Specification F9/40 for a jet-powered interceptor fighter. An order for eight prototypes and 20 production F1s was placed in September 1941. The Halford H1 powered prototype DG206 made its first flight on 5 March 1943. Production Meteor F1s EE210-229 were fitted with improved Rolls-Royce W2B/23 Welland engines and the first delivery to an operational squadron was to No 616 Sqn at Culmhead on 12 July 1944. Meteors of various marks (F3, F4, F8, FR9 and PR10) served with RAF squadrons until July 1961. The T7 was a two-seat tandem trainer with a framed, hinged canopy. A tandem-seat night fighter version was developed by Armstrong Whitworth and produced as the Meteor NF11-14.
Survivors: Although there are many examples of the Meteor preserved in museums and collections around the world there are relatively few in flying condition. In the UK there is a flyable Meteor F8 operated by Adrian Gjertsen and a Meteor NF11 with Jet Heritage at Bournemouth. Several more Meteors (Mks 7, 8 and 14) are on long-term restoration to fly again.
Recognition: Low-set wings with a wide centre-section integral with the fuselage and including the two jet nacelles and landing-gear units. Outer wing sections have increased taper and rounded tips (some later versions had clipped wings). Oval-section fuselage. Blister-type cockpit canopy forward of the leading edge of the wings. Engine nacelles above and below wing with extended jet pipe to rear. Tailplane mounted near top of fin with bullet fairing at front.

Grumman TBF/TBM Avenger

Single-engined torpedo bomber/ASW/AEW aircraft

Powerplant: One 1,305kW (1,750hp) Wright R-2600-20 Double Cyclone radial engine

Span: 16.5m (54ft 2in)

Length: 12.2m (40ft 0in)

Maximum speed: 445km/h (278mph)

First aircraft flown: 1 August 1941

Above: *Based in France this Grumman TBM Avenger is painted in RN D-Day colours.* ***PRM***

History: The Avenger became a key torpedo and attack aircraft in the Pacific War. It made its operational début in mid-1942 in the Battle of Midway. The slightly modified TBM-3 was introduced in April 1944 and many had no turret; all had strengthened wings for rockets or radar pods. The TBM-3E was equipped for ASW search and attack and the TBM-3W had an airborne early warning radar. Three versions of the aircraft were supplied under Lend-Lease to the Fleet Air Arm for bombing, strike and anti-submarine duties. The Avenger returned to front-line FAA service in May 1953, equipping five anti-submarine squadrons until 1955, under the Mutual Defence Assistance Programme.

Survivors: A large number of Avengers have been kept in flying condition by private owners in North America. There are two airworthy TBMs in Europe — one in France and the other based at Duxford.

Recognition: Mid-set wings with a rectangular centre-section and equal-tapered folding outer sections. Long 'glasshouse' cockpit canopy with the pilot's position over leading edge of wing. Most early models had dorsal turret and ventral hatch gun position to rear of wing. Fully enclosed torpedo/bomb bay. Tall fin and rudder with dorsal fillet. Tailplane set on top of rear fuselage.

Grumman F6F Hellcat

Single-engined, single-seat carrier-based fighter

Powerplant: One 1,504kW (2,000hp) Pratt & Whitney R-2800-10W 18-cylinder, two-row air-cooled radial engine

Span: 13.05m (42ft 10in)

Length: 10.24m (33ft 7in)

Maximum speed: 612.9km/h (380mph)

First aircraft flown: 26 June 1942

History: Designed by Grumman aircraft as a private-venture replacement for the Wildcat, the F6F had considerably more power but other than its low-set wing, closely resembled its predecessor. This allowed the main landing gear to retract into the centre-section rather than the lower fuselage. In 1943 the first of 1,182 Lend-Lease deliveries were made to the Fleet Air Arm of the Hellcat I/II. By 1944 the Hellcat, together with the F4U Corsair, had become standard US Navy equipment throughout the Pacific. A total of 7,870 Hellcats were produced.

Right: *Grumman F6F Hellcat operated by The Fighter Collection at Duxford.* ***PRM***

Survivors: There are 28 surviving F6Fs of which one-third are currently believed to be airworthy. One Hellcat (G-BTCC/N10CN) is operated by the Fighter Collection at Duxford.

Recognition: Short fuselage with low-set folding wings which have equal tapering chord with square wing tips. Small cockpit canopy, tapering sharply to rear fuselage. Tailplane, with rounded tips set midway at rear of fuselage. Inward-retracting main wheels and retractable tailwheel. Large radial engine with three-blade propeller.

Grumman F7F Tigercat

Single-seat, twin-engined, carrier-based fighter-bomber

Powerplant: Two 1,579kW (2,100hp) Pratt & Whitney R-2800-22W 18-cylinder, two-row air-cooled radial engines

Span: 15.6m (51ft 6in)

Length: 13.8m (45ft 4in)

Maximum speed: 701 km/h (435mph)

First aircraft flown: December 1943

Above: *One of four Tigercats currently airworthy in the USA, this F7F is based at Oakland, California.* ***PRM***

History: The Tigercat was designed for operation from the new 45,000 ton carriers of the USS *Midway* class. It was the US Navy's first twin built in production quantities and the first carrier-based fighter to operate with a tricycle undercarriage. Although classified as a fighter, the F7F was designed to operate in a tactical ground-support role, for which it was heavily armed. Deliveries began in April 1944, but operational problems and changing requirements led to restrictions in the production programme. The F7F-2N, of which 65 were built, was a two-seat night fighter. The Tigercat arrived too late for operational service in World War 2 but saw service with US Marine Squadrons postwar, but was soon displaced by the new jets.

Survivors: There are 14 surviving Tigercats of which six are believed to be airworthy and two more are under restoration to fly.

Recognition: Short broad-chord wing, with straight leading edge and square tips, and two large engines slung in large nacelles beneath the folding wings. Very narrow fuselage. Upper rear fuselage curved upwards to rounded fin with straight trailing edge. Arrester hook under rear fuselage. Tailplane set midway on fin, with swept leading edge and straight trailing edge. Wings feature noticeable anhedral. Retractable tricycle undercarriage with long nosewheel leg.

Grumman F8F Bearcat

Single-engined, single-seat, carrier-borne interceptor fighter
Powerplant: One 1,579kW (2,100hp) Pratt & Whitney R-2800-34W 18-cylinder, two-row air-cooled radial engine
Span: 7.87m (35ft 10in)
Length: 8.61m (28ft 3in)
Maximum speed: 679km/h (421mph)
First aircraft flown: 21 August 1944
History: The Bearcat was a smaller, faster and more powerful development of the Hellcat. It was too late to see combat in World War 2 but it played an important part in the Indo-China war with the French Armée de l'Air and Royal Thai Air Force. Re-equipment of US Navy squadrons continued throughout 1946 and 1947 and 24 units received the type by 1948 from the 770 built. Some were built as F8F-1N night fighters, with radome under one wing. An improved F8F-2 was introduced in 1948 with 20mm cannon, revised engine cowling and taller fin and rudder, of which 365 were delivered.
Survivors: There are more than 30 surviving F8Fs of which 13 are flyable. Although most of them are based in the USA, F8F-2P NX700HL is operated by the Fighter Collection at Duxford.
Recognition: Low-wing monoplane with a short, deep fuselage. Tear-drop sliding cockpit cover, set level with trailing edge of wing. Dorsal fillet to upright fin and rudder. Straight leading edge to folding wings, small forward fillet at base of leading edge. Inward-retracting main wheels and retractable tailwheel. Slightly swept leading edge to tailplane, with straight trailing edge. Protruding four cannon barrels in wing leading edge.

Grumman FM-2/F4F Wildcat

Single-engined, single-seat, carrier-borne fighter
Powerplant: One 895kW (1,200hp) Pratt & Whitney R-1820-86 Twin Wasp radial engine
Span: 11.58m (38ft 0in)
Length: 8.76m (28ft 9in)
Maximum speed: 512km/h (318mph)
First aircraft flown: 2 September 1937
History: The Wildcat was planned as a biplane, but then recast as a portly monoplane. The type, supplied to the British Fleet Air Arm from 1940, was initially known as the Martlet, and served aboard the small escort carriers. A very manoeuvrable aircraft that could turn inside any aircraft it met. The Wildcat was decisive in limiting the superiority of Japanese fighters in the Pacific theatre — despite its modest speed it was agile, heavily armed and well protected. The F4F-3 was the initial model, FM-4 the definitive fighter and known as the FM-1/FM-2 when built by General Motors. The Wildcat IV was the British version of the F4F-4, the Wildcat V was the FM-1 and Wildcat VI the British version of the FM-2.
Survivors: An FM-2 Wildcat (N4845V) is operated by The Fighter Collection at Duxford and there is another in the hands of the Amicale Jean Salis at La Ferte Alais in France. There are 12 Wildcats active in the USA and two in Australasia, from a total of 40 known to exist around the world.
Recognition: Mid-wing cantilever monoplane. Short stubby oval fuselage. Folding wings. Main wheels retract into the sides of the front fuselage. Fixed tailwheel. Small enclosed cockpit, tapering sharply to the rear. Wings of equal taper with square tips. Curved fillet at front base of upright fin and rudder. Tailplane, with square tips, set at base of fin above fuselage.

Above: *Recently restored Grumman F8F-2 Bearcat owned by the Confederate Air Force and based in California.* **PRM**

Above: *Grumman FM-2 Wildcat flying from Duxford with The Fighter Collection.* **PRM**

Hawker Hart/Hind

Single-engined two-seat day bomber biplane
Powerplant: One 417.6kW (560hp) Rolls-Royce Kestrel IIIS V-12 liquid-cooled engine
Span: 11.35m (37ft 3in)
Length: 8.93m (29ft 4in)
Maximum speed: 298km/h (184mph)
First aircraft flown: June 1928
History: The Hart was designed at Kingston in 1927 to meet RAF Specification 12/26. The Hawker Hart family spawned a number of variants. The Demon was a two-seat fighter version with a supercharged Kestrel; The Osprey was a two-seat fighter for the Fleet Air Arm; the Hardy a general purpose aircraft; the Audax an army co-operation aircraft. The final major model was the Hind bomber of 1934. The RAF received 527 Hinds and over 130 were exported. The RAF also received 507 Hart Trainers and 164 Hind Trainers.
Survivors: There is a single airworthy Hind with the Shuttleworth Collection at Old Warden and a Demon and Audax on long-term restoration to fly. Other non-flying Harts and Hart Trs are preserved in museums.
Recognition: Single-bay biplane having unequal-span staggered wings, with round tips. Top wing is slightly swept whereas the leading edge of the lower plane is straight. Streamlined pointed nose housing the Kestrel engine, with large spinner and prominent exhaust stubs. Pilot seated in open cockpit above trailing edge of lower wing. V-struts for undercarriage legs. Braced tailplane.

Above: *This former Afghan Air Force Hawker Hind is flown by The Shuttleworth Collection.* ***PRM***

Hawker Hunter F4/F6/T7/GA11

Single-engined jet fighter and two-seat dual trainer
Data for Hunter GA11

Powerplant: One 42.3kN (9,500lb st) Rolls-Royce Avon RA7/RA21/RA28 turbojet
Span: 10.26m (33ft 8in)
Length: 13.98m (45ft 10.5in)
Maximum speed: 1,144km/h (710mph)
First aircraft flown: 20 June 1951

Above: *One of the single-seat Hawker Hunter GA11s privately owned at Exeter.* ***PRM***

Below: *This privately owned two-seat Hawker Hunter T7 shows its longer nose and humped-back appearance.* ***PRM***

History: Designed to meet Specification F3/48 for a Meteor F8 replacement, the Hawker P1067 was ordered in prototype form in June 1948. Three years later the prototype WB188 made its first flight from Boscombe Down. The first of 140 production Hunter F1s WT555 was airborne on 16 May 1953 and deliveries of this Avon 100 powered version were made to Nos 43, 54 and 222 Squadrons. The F4 had an improved thrust Avon, increased fuel capacity and points for underwing stores. Over 350 F4s were built and many were later modified to T7, T8 and GA11 standard. The first Hunter F6 was flown on 22 January 1954 and again an uprated Avon gave an improved performance. Nearly 400 F6s were delivered, the first squadron to receive them being No 74 Squadron at the end of 1956. On 9 July 1957 the last new-built Hunter F6 XK156 was flown. Total Hunter production was 1,985 including 445 made in Belgium and Holland.

Survivors: With the retirement of the last Hunters operated by the RN and Swiss Air Force, a large number have passed to civilian operators across Europe, North America and South Africa. In the UK Jet Heritage at Bournemouth and Classic Jets at Exeter both look after mixed fleets of six airworthy single and two-seat Hunters.

Recognition: Deep-chord swept wings set midway up the long, slim fuselage. The glazed cockpit canopy is near to the nose, well ahead of leading edge of wing. Engine intakes in wing roots. Jet pipe at rear fuselage extremity. Swept tail fin and rudder. Swept tailplane mounted half-way up fin. Often seen with underwing drop tanks.

Hawker Hurricane

Single-engined, single-seat fighter
Powerplant: One 768kW (1,030hp) Rolls-Royce Merlin II in-line piston engine
Span: 12.19m (40ft 0in)
Length: 9.75m (32ft 0in)
Maximum speed: 511km/h (318mph)
First aircraft flown: 6 November 1935
History: Designed by Sydney Camm in 1934 as a private venture to meet Specification F5/34, the Hurricane was the first monoplane fighter to join the RAF when it entered service with No 111 Squadron at Northolt in December 1937. By the outbreak of war the RAF had nearly 500 Hurricanes on strength with 18 squadrons and a year later in the Battle of Britain nearly 2,500 had been delivered and 32 fighter squadrons were flying the aircraft. The improved Merlin XX engine with a two-stage supercharger was fitted to the MkII Hurricane which entered service in late 1940. Subsequently the Hurricane was switched to fighter-bombing and tank-busting. Total production was 12,780 in Britain and 1,451 in Canada.
Survivors: A total of 60 Hurricanes are known to exist of which six are flyable and a further five are under restoration to fly. Four of the fliers are based in the UK — Battle of Britain Memorial Flight, IWM/Shuttleworth Collection (the world's only Sea Hurricane), The Fighter Collection and a privately owned example; and one each in Canada (Canadian Warbird Heritage) and the USA (Santa Monica Museum).
Recognition: Low-set wing with centre-section of parallel chord and thickness and two tapering outer sections. Deep fuselage and enclosed pilot's cockpit, with sliding 'birdcage' canopy, over the wing. Typical Hawker rounded fin and rudder. Tailplane mounted high on rear fuselage. Main wheels retract inwards into wings; fixed tailwheel.

Top: *Hawker Hurricane IIC operated by The Battle of Britain Memorial Flight at RAF Coningsby.* ***DJM***

Above: *The Fighter Collection's ex-Canadian Hawker Hurricane XII.* ***APM***

Hawker Sea Fury

Single-engined naval fighter-bomber

Powerplant: One 1,849kW (2,480hp) Bristol Centaurus 18-cylinder two-row sleeve-valve radial engine

Span: 11.69m (38ft 4.75in)

Length: 10.56m (34ft 8in)

Maximum speed: 740km/h (460mph)

First aircraft flown: 21 February 1945

History: The Sea Fury was a development of the Tempest II, via the Fury I, that was designed to Specification F2/43 for a high-speed fighter aircraft powered by a Centaurus engine. It was the ultimate British combat aircraft to have a single piston engine. The first production Sea Fury FB10 was airborne on 30 September 1946. After 50 had been delivered, entering service with 807 Squadron in August 1947, 615 Sea Fury FB11s were built. Sea Furies were involved in the Korean War flying from the carriers *Ocean*, *Theseus* and *Glory*, as well as the Australian carrier *Sydney*. The first of a number of MiG 15s was shot down by an 802 Sqn aircraft on 9 August 1952. From 1953 the Sea Fury was replaced by the Sea Hawk, being relegated to RNVR Squadrons until 1957 and finally used by the Fleet Requirements Unit at Hurn until 1963. Total production was 860, of which the FAA received 615.

Survivors: A total of over 60 Sea Furies and ex-Iraqi Air Force Furies currently exist, of which 36 are potentially airworthy. Nearly all of these aircraft are operated in the USA, while just four are based in the UK.

Recognition: Low-wing monoplane with thin high-speed laminar-flow wings which are elliptical in plan form with squared-off tips. Dihedral on the outer section of the wings. Oval-shaped fuselage. Single-piece moulded 'blister' type canopy enclosing the cockpit. Large radial engine with five-blade propeller and large spinner. Tall angular tail fin and rudder. Tailplane set high on rear fuselage.

Top: *This Hawker Sea Fury FB11, painted in Royal Australian Navy markings, is based in California.* ***PRM***

Above: *This Florida-based Hawker Fury FB10 (ex-Iraqi AF) has wing-tip smoke canisters for airshow performances.* ***PRM***

Hawker Siddeley Gnat T1

Single-engined two-seat jet trainer

Powerplant: One 18.84kN (4,230lb st) Bristol Siddeley Orpheus 100 turbojet

Span: 7.31m (24ft 0in)

Length: 9.67m (31ft 9in)

Maximum speed: 1,024km/h (635mph)

First aircraft flown: 18 July 1955 (F1); 31 August 1959 (T1)

Above: *One of the Hawker Siddeley Gnat T1s operated by Kennet Aviation from Cranfield.* ***PRM***

Below: *This privately owned Gnat T1 is painted in the RAF Yellowjacks display team markings.* ***DJM***

History: W. E. Petter designed a lightweight fighter that was developed by Folland Aircraft at Hamble to produce the Fo139 Midge that was first flown on 11 August 1954. Powered by a 1,640lb st Viper jet engine this tiny single-seat fighter attracted a good deal of interest and the Fo141 Gnat, basically the Midge refined, with a 4,400lb St Bristol Siddeley Orpheus, was first flown in July 1955. The RAF ordered over 100 of the larger two-seat Gnat trainers built by Hawker Siddeley. They were used as advanced pilot training aircraft from 1962 to 1979.

Survivors: Since being replaced by the Hawk, ex-RAF Gnats have been sold to private buyers in the UK and North America. In 1995 there were 15 airworthy Gnats, of which one-third are operated in the UK. Kennet Aviation at Cranfield operates two Gnats, while there are two others based at North Weald.

Recognition: Shoulder-wing monoplane with short swept wings. Low-set swept tailplane. Small oblong engine intakes set in fuselage sides just ahead of leading edge of wings. Single-piece cockpit canopy over the tandem seats. Pronounced dorsal spine from rear of cockpit to base of swept fin. Main undercarriage doors act as air brakes and retract into the fuselage.

Heinkel He111/CASA 2.111

Twin-engined medium bomber
Data for: CASA 2.111
Powerplant: Two CASA built 1,193kW (1,600hp) Rolls-Royce Merlin 500/29 engines
Span: 22.6m (74ft 1.75in)
Length: 16.6m (54ft 6in)
Maximum speed: 415km/h (258mph)
First aircraft flown: 24 February 1935
History: The He111 served with the Condor Legion in the Spanish Civil War and was advanced by the standards of the mid-1930s, being faster than most single-seat fighters. Its production life spanned nine years with over 5,200 built by 1944. In 1941 the Spanish Government acquired a licence to build the He111H-16 at the CASA plant at Tablada. Production of the CASA 2.111A powered by Jumo 211F engines, and the 2.111-B/D with 1,193kW (1,610hp) Rolls-Royce Merlin 500-29s continued until 1956. The last CASA 2.111s in service with the Spanish Air Force were withdrawn in 1976 at Cuatro Vientos and subsequently sold to museums and private operators.

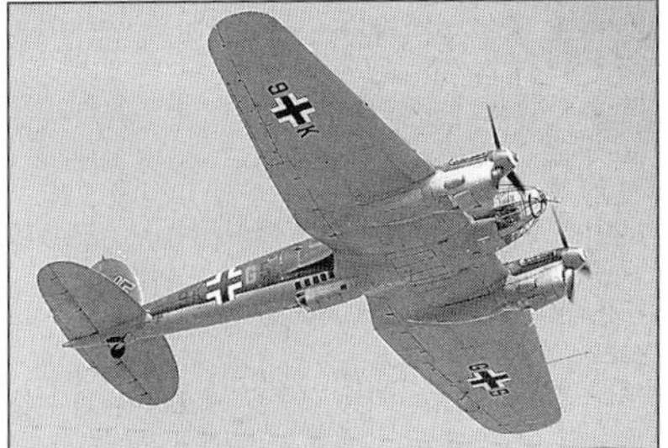

Top and above: *The world's only airworthy CASA 2.111D is owned by the Confederate Air Force and based in Arizona.* ***PRM***

Survivors: Currently there is only one example (an ex-Spanish Air Force CASA 2.111) airworthy. This is owned by the Confederate Air Force and based in Arizona. The Old Flying Machine Company at Duxford plans to add another example to its fleet after restoration has been completed.
Recognition: Low-wing monoplane with elliptical wings and rounded tips. Prominent cut-out at trailing edge wing root. Oval-section fuselage. Completely glazed nose which incorporates cockpit and crew stations. Nose is in line with the two engine spinners. Sharply tapered rear fuselage and low set elliptical tailplane. Semi-elliptical fin and rudder. Rear upper and lower ventral gun positions.

Hunting-Percival Provost

Single-engined, two-seat basic trainer
Powerplant: One 410kW (550hp) Alvis Leonides 126 radial piston engine
Span: 10.72m (35ft 2in)
Length: 8.74m (28ft 8in)
Maximum speed: 322km/h (201mph)
First aircraft flown: 23 February 1950
History: The P56 Provost was designed to Specification T16/48 by Percival Aircraft prior to it becoming part of the Hunting Group in 1954. It was selected by the RAF as its basic trainer in 1951, when an initial order for 200 was placed. The first aircraft were delivered to the Central Flying School in April 1953 and gradually replaced the Prentice. The last of 387 Provosts was taken on charge on 29 March 1956. Replacement for the Provost T1 with RAF flying schools came with the introduction of the Jet Provost, and the last Provosts were sold by the RAF in 1969.
Survivors: There are 10 flyable Provosts from a total of 30 located in the UK. Other examples survive in Australia and North America.
Recognition: Low-wing monoplane, the wings having equal taper with square tips. Long, faired, fixed main undercarriage legs that are canted forwards. Large radial engine. Sliding cockpit canopy over side-by-side seating. Tall angular fin and rudder with square top. Square-tipped tailplane at fuselage extremity, to the rear of fin. Fixed tailwheel at extreme rear.

Hunting-Percival Prince/Sea Prince/Pembroke

Twin-engined light utility/transport aircraft
Data for Hunting-Percival Pembroke C1
Powerplant: Two 417.6kW (560hp) Alvis Leonides 127 nine-cylinder radial piston engines
Span: 19.66m (64ft 6in)
Length: 14.02m (46ft 0in)
Maximum speed: 360km/h (224mph)
First aircraft flown: 13 May 1948 (Prince); 20 November 1952 (Pembroke)
History: The Percival P50 Prince was flown in prototype form powered by two 388kW (520hp) Alvis Leonides engines. The Prince 2 appeared with design improvements to give higher speed and greater all-up weight. On 24 March 1950 the first of a quartet of Sea Prince C1s was flown at Luton. It was followed by 42 Sea Prince T1s, the first of which was flown on 28 June 1951. These observer trainers remained in service with the RN at Culdrose until 1979. The RAF ordered 45 of the larger Pembrokes, entering service as communications and photographic aircraft in 1953 and remaining operational for the next 35 years.
Survivors: A number of Sea Princes and Pembrokes were sold to private owners in the UK and USA when they were retired from military service. Single examples of each are currently airworthy in Britain, with a Prince and Sea Prince under active restoration.
Recognition: High-wing monoplane with low-slung radial engines and nacelles extending to the rear of the trailing edge. Long rounded nose with a curved underside to fuselage. Four rectangular passenger windows on each side of the fuselage. Entry door at rear on port side. Rounded fin and rudder with small dorsal extension. Tailplane set at base of fin.

Above: *Hunting-Percival Provost T1 based at Cranfield with Kennet Aviation.* ***PRM***

Above: *A former RAF Hunting-Percival Pembroke C1, now privately owned, retains its former markings of No 60 Sqn.* ***PRM***

Hunting (BAC) Jet Provost

Single-engined, two-seat jet trainer
Data for BAC Jet Provost T5
Powerplant: One 11.13kN (2,500lb st) Rolls-Royce Viper Mk202 turbojet
Span: 10.77m (35ft 4in)
Length: 10.27m (33ft 8.5in)
Maximum speed: 708km/h (440mph)
First aircraft flown: 26 June 1954
History: A development of the piston-engined Provost basic trainer, the jet-powered Provost was designed as a private venture by Hunting-Percival. The RAF saw the potential for all-through jet training and on 27 March 1953 ordered 10 of these aircraft for evaluation. The prototype Jet Provost T1 was first flown at Luton just over a year later. Nine aircraft were delivered to No 2 FTS at Hullavington where they were used to train several courses of pilots. The type was adopted by the RAF as a basic trainer and first deliveries of the production Jet Provost T3 commenced in June 1959. It was followed by the higher powered T4 in November 1961. A further development, the BAC Jet Provost T5, had a pressurised cockpit, longer nose and a Viper 202 engine. The Strikemaster was a dual-role light attack/trainer with a 15.2kN (3,410lb st) Viper 535.

Top: *The sole airworthy Hunting Jet Provost T1 is flown by Kennet Aviation at Cranfield.* ***PRM***

Above: *This pre-production BAC Jet Provost T5 is now privately owned at North Weald.* ***PRM***

Survivors: With replacement by the Tucano, a large number of RAF Jet Provosts have been sold to private operators in the UK and USA. Kennet Aviation has the only surviving airworthy Jet Provost T1. There are currently 12 Jet Provost T3/T4s flyable in the UK and a handful of T5s, most of which are based at North Weald.
Recognition: Short fuselage with small, rounded fin and rectangular low-set tailplane. A bubble canopy over side-by-side seats, set forward of the wings, with small semi-circular air intakes on either side of the fuselage. Low-set, unswept wings, with tip tanks carried by most versions.

Above: *This Junkers Ju52/3m is demonstrated across Europe by its owner, the German airline Lufthansa.* ***PRM***

Junkers Ju52/CASA 352

Three-engined, passenger and freight transport
Powerplant: Three 618.9kW (830hp) BMW132T radial engines
Span: 29.25m (95ft 11.5in)
Length: 18.9m (62ft 0in)
Maximum speed: 305km/h (190mph)
First aircraft flown: May 1932
History: The Ju52/3m was built as a 15-17 seat passenger airliner that sold widely and made up 75% of the Lufthansa fleet. It was mass-produced for the emergent Luftwaffe as a transport and paratroop carrier, serving on every front on which Nazi Germany fought. The Auntie Ju or Iron Annie as it was nicknamed, was kept in full production throughout the war. Some 4,845 Ju52/3ms were built in Germany alone and its production continued after World War 2 by Société Amiot in France as the AAC1 (400 were completed in 1947). The final 170 were built in Spain as CASA 352Ls, powered by 559kW (750hp) ENMA Beta radial engines. These were operated by the Spanish Air Force as multi-role transports until 1975.
Survivors: A small number of Ju52/CASA 352Ls remain airworthy — currently one in Texas with the Confederate Air Force, two in Switzerland, and one in South Africa and Germany. Two further examples are under restoration to fly again.
Recognition: Three-engined monoplane. Rectangular section fuselage with pronounced domed decking and corrugated panels. Dorsal gun position on most versions. Angular fin and rudder. Wings of equal taper, with the wing-mounted engines splayed slightly outwards. Elevators extend beyond the edge of the tailplane. Fixed taildragger undercarriage; main wheels sometimes have spats. Small glazed 'birdcage' cockpit and six oblong windows on each side of fuselage. Entry door, with glazed panel, on port side.

Above: *Confederate Air Force Lockheed PV-2 Harpoon based in Louisiana.* **PRM**

Below: *A former US Navy PV-2 Harpoon owned by the American Military Heritage Foundation in Indianapolis.* **PRM**

Lockheed Hudson/ Ventura/Harpoon

Twin-engined maritime reconnaissance/torpedo bomber
Data for PV-2 Harpoon
Powerplant: Two 1,491kW (2,000hp) Pratt & Whitney R-2800-31 Double Wasp 18-cylinder radial engines
Span: 22.83m (74ft 11in)
Length: 15.86m (52ft 0.5in)
Maximum speed: 454km/h (282mph)
First aircraft flown: Hudson — 29 July 1937; Ventura — 31 July 1941; Ventura (PV-1) 3 November 1942; Harpoon (PV-2) 3 December 1943
History: The Hudson was a military derivative of the prewar Lockheed 14 12-seat airliner. The RAF obtained 200 for general reconnaissance use, replacing Ansons. Subsequently the RAF ordered 875 Venturas, derived from the Lockheed 18 Lodestar airliner with a longer fuselage and a rear ventral gun position than the Hudson. It proved a mediocre bomber and deliveries stopped at 300. The US Navy and USAAF received some 600 PV-1 Venturas/B-34 Lexingtons. The redesigned PV-2 Harpoon with larger wings, new tail and up to 10 0.5in guns, was operated by the US Navy during the last year of the war.
Survivors: Examples of the Hudson, Ventura and Harpoon are all actively flying in the USA, mostly in the hands of the Confederate Air Force and similar warbird museums and collections.
Recognition: Mid-wing monoplane, wings of constant taper and with rounded wing tips. Rectangular tailplane with twin fins and rudders at the outer extremity. Elliptical-section fuselage. Solid nose and dorsal turret half-way along fuselage. Cranked ventral fuselage housing gun position. Five fixed guns in nose. Large bulged weapons bay with fully enclosing doors.

Lockheed T-33/Canadair T-33A-N Silver Star

Single-turbojet, two-seat trainer
Powerplant: One 23.16kN (5,200lb st Allison J33-35 (T-33); or one 22.71kN (5,100lb st) Rolls-Royce Nene 10 turbojet (Canadair T-33A-N)
Span: 11.85m (38ft 10.5in)
Length: 11.50m (37ft 9in)
Maximum speed: 975km/h (606mph)
First aircraft flown: 8 January 1944
History: The T-33 was developed from the Lockheed P-80 (later F-80) Shooting Star. The T-33 was for 20 years the world's most widely used jet trainer; the whole programme stemmed from an F-80C taken from the production line and given an extra section of fuselage with a second seat, covered by a long clamshell canopy. Lockheed delivered some 5,820 trainers, including 217 T-1A Sea Stars for the US Navy. Canadair built 656 CL-30 Silver Stars powered by a Rolls-Royce Nene engine, serving with a number of NATO air forces and the RCAF as the CT-33.
Survivors: Over 150 T-33s are known to exist, of which one-third are potentially airworthy in collections and private owners' hands in the USA. There is only one flyable example based in the UK, at Duxford.
Recognition: Low-set wings of equal taper with noticeable dihedral. Wing-tip tanks fitted which incorporate small fins. Scooped engine intakes in sides of fuselage ahead of wing leading edge. Long one-piece canopy over tandem seats. Narrow fin and rudder with front dorsal extension. Swept tailplane set high on rear fuselage above the jet pipe.

Top: *The Coleman Warbird Museum's Lockheed T-33A that is based in Texas.* ***PRM***

Above: *This Lockheed T-33A-N is operated by the Old Flying Machine Company from Duxford.* ***PRM***

Lockheed P-38 Lightning

Above: Lockheed P-38J Lightning based at Duxford with The Fighter Collection. **DJM**

Below: An unusual three-place Lockheed P-38JLM Lightning restored by the Confederate Air Force at San Marcos, Texas. **PRM**

Twin-engined, long-range fighter
Powerplant: Two 1,133.4kW (1,520hp) Allison V-1710 twelve-cylinder Vee liquid-cooled engines
Span: 15.86m (52ft 0in)
Length: 11.53m (37ft 10in)
Maximum speed: 666km/h (414mph)
First aircraft flown: 27 January 1939
History: The P-38 was the only US fighter built before World War 2 still to be in production on VJ Day. Designed as a twin-engined long-range fighter, it had a twin-boom layout and engines with exhaust-driven turbo-superchargers. Deliveries began in July 1941. It was used in all US combat theatres as a high- and low-altitude fighter, escort, fighter-bomber, photographic reconnaissance, low-level attack and smoke screen layer. Most extensively built was the P-38L that carried rocket projectiles beneath the outer wings. Some were converted as three-seat 'Pathfinders'. A total of 9,923 P-38s were delivered to the USAAF. The last aircraft was retired in 1949.
Survivors: There are more than 30 P-38s surviving around the world, with eight currently airworthy in the USA and one in the UK (P-38J Lightning NX3145X/42-67543 operated by The Fighter Collection from Duxford painted in 20th FG USAAF colours as California Cutie). Four P-38s are being restored/rebuilt in the USA.
Recognition: Mid-set wings that taper in chord and thickness with round tips. Twin booms extend from the two engines to the twin oval tail fins. Bulges in booms, housing the engine's coolant radiators, to rear of trailing edge of wing. Pointed nose which houses four 0.50in machine guns, with centre nacelle housing the cockpit over leading edge of wing. Tricycle undercarriage. Three-blade contra-handed propellers.

Above: *A UK-based Max Holste MH1521M Broussard painted in French Air Force North African markings.* ***PRM***

Below: *Former French Air Force Broussard that is based in the UK.* ***PRM***

Max Holste Broussard

Single-engined, light utility transport
Powerplant: One 335kW (450hp) Pratt & Whitney R-985-AN-1 nine-cylinder radial piston engine
Span: 13.75m (45ft 1.25in)
Length: 8.65m (28ft 4.5in)
Maximum speed: 270km/h (168mph)
First aircraft flown: 17 November 1952
History: The MH1521 Broussard was designed as a light high-wing cabin monoplane, derived from the experimental MH152 air observation post. It was ordered in quantity by the French Air Force as a six-seat general utility and transport and liaison aircraft. The rear four seats are removable for carrying freight. It was also flown by the air arms of 11 other countries.

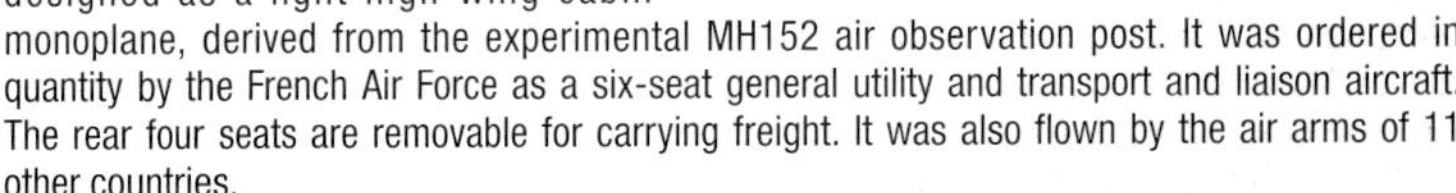

Survivors: A number of Broussards remain airworthy in Europe, with the majority in France. There are three flyable Broussards in Britain and the USA.
Recognition: High-wing monoplane with braced constant chord wings and rounded tips. Fixed main wheel struts fixed to bottom of wing struts. Twin fins and rudders. Large radial engine with exhaust underneath. Raked windscreen ahead of wing leading edge. Four windows on either side of the fuselage and wide door on port side.

Above: *This RAF-owned Messerschmitt Bf109G is kept airworthy, for the time being, with the Imperial War Museum at Duxfprd.* ***PRM***

Below: *One of two Daimler Benz-powered Bf109Gs that are currently airworthy in Europe.* ***DJM***

Messerschmitt Bf109

Single-engined fighter
Data for Bf109G
Powerplant: One 1,099kW (1,475hp) Daimler Benz DB601N inverted V-12 liquid-cooled engine
Span: 9.92m (32ft 6.5in)
Length: 8.84m (29ft 0.5in)
Maximum speed: 621km/h (386mph)
First aircraft flown: September 1935
History: Nearly 35,000 Messerschmitt Bf109s were produced between 1936 and 1945, more than any other combat aircraft in World War 2. It was a major participant in the Spanish Civil War and already a well-proven combat fighter by September 1939. Initially the Bf109 was powered by a Junkers Jumo 210A, while the first version to be mass-produced, the Bf109E Emil had a Daimler Benz DB601A of 782.9kW (1,050hp). The Bf109F with a DB601N engine entered service in 1941, the DB605A-1 powered Bf109G Gustav followed a year later and the ultimate Bf109K with its 1,155.8kW (1,550hp) DB605 ASCM/DCM joined the Luftwaffe in late 1944. The airframe was improved to give better speed, manoeuvrability and weapons capability. The Spanish Hispano Aviacien flew its first licence-built aircraft (HA1109) in March 1945 and in 1953 switched to the Rolls-Royce Merlin engine to produce the HA-1112 Buchon (Pigeon), the last being produced in 1956.
Survivors: There are a total of eight Bf109/HA1112s potentially airworthy, of which three are powered by the Daimler Benz DB601 engine. In addition, there are at least 60 surviving examples, of which eight are currently under restoration to fly.
Recognition: Low-wing monoplane with straight leading edges to its wing and rounded wing tips. Engine coolant-radiators, one on each side of the fuselage, partly buried under the surface of wings. Oval-section fuselage. 'Birdcage', small, hinged cockpit canopy. Rounded fin and rudder with the tailplane set midway up fin. Main undercarriage retracts outwards.

Mikoyan-Gurevich MiG-15/17/19

Single-jet-engined fighter and two-seat trainer
Data for MiG-15

Above: *This Polish-built MiG-15UTI Mongol is operated by The Old Flying Machine Company at Duxford.* ***PRM***

Powerplant: One 22.26kN (5,005lb st) RD-45F turbojet engine (based on Rolls-Royce Nene)
Span: 10.08m (33ft 0.75in)
Length: 11.05m (36ft 3.25in)
Maximum speed: 1,075km/h (668mph)
First aircraft flown: MiG-15 — 30 December 1947; MiG-17 — 1952; MiG-19 — September 1953
History: The Mikoyan design bureau used the Rolls-Royce Nene jet engine, supplied by Britain, to power the I-310 fighter prototype. Put into production the following year as the MiG-15, it proved to be one of the world's best swept-wing fighters of the period. Several thousand were built and it saw combat service in Korea. The MiG-17, featuring an afterburning engine, replaced it in 1953. The MiG-19 had a further improved engine and carried first-generation radar-homing missiles instead of guns. By the end of the 1950s the MiG-19 was phased out in favour of the MiG-21, but continued to be licence-built in China. The -UTI versions were two-seat trainers.
Survivors: There are examples of the MiG-15 (mainly Polish-built WSK SBLim-2A two-seaters) flying in the UK (G-OMIG/6247 operated by The Old Flying Machine Company at Duxford), in Australia and the USA where there are also two flyable MiG-17s.
Recognition: Mid-set, sharply swept wings and tailplane. Short blunt nose for bifurcated jet intake. Short stubby fuselage. Small cockpit set ahead of leading edge of wing. Jet pipe exits at rear fuselage under tail fin. Swept fin and rudder with the tailplane set high on it. Twin wing fences on top of each wing. Retractable air brakes at rear of fuselage.

Mikoyan-Gurevich MiG-21

Single-jet-engined air defence fighter
Powerplant: One 64.73kN (14,500lb st) Turmansky R-13-300 turbojet with afterburner
Span: 7.15m (23ft 5.5in)
Length: 15.76m (51ft 8.5in)
Maximum speed: Mach 2.1
First aircraft flown: 1955
History: The MiG-21 (NATO codename Fishbed) was developed on the basis of experience of air combat in the Korean War. In the 1980s it became the most widely used fighter in the world. Continuous development kept the MiG-21 in production for 25 years and it was ultimately flown by 33 air arms. The later MiG-21F was equipped with infra-red homing air-to-air missiles. In comparison with other Mach 2 fighters, the MiG-21 is a light and refined aircraft with moderate engine thrust — but because of good airframe dynamics it could reach Mach 2. To improve landing/take-off characteristics and rate of turn Mikoyan introduced laminar-flow control on the MiG-21.
Survivors: While the MiG-21 remains in front-line service with many air arms, there are two dozen examples in the West of which about a quarter are airworthy. There are two MiG-21s being rebuilt to flying condition in the UK.
Recognition: Delta-shaped mid-wing with 60° sweep to leading edge. Swept tailplane mounted on centre of rear fuselage. Deep fuselage of same depth throughout its length. Nose engine intake incorporating weapon radar in central cone. Sleek cockpit with pronounced dorsal spine behind canopy. Large swept fin and rudder. Pronounced ventral fuselage strake at rear.

Top: *Former Czechoslovak Air Force Mikoyan-Gurevich MiG-21PF.* ***PRM***

Above: *This MiG-21MF was presented to the RAF Benevolent Fund and was initially based at Boscombe Down.* ***PRM***

Above: *Based at Shoreham, this restored Miles Magister 1 is privately owned.* ***PRM***

Miles Hawk Trainer III/Magister

Single-engined, two-seat primary trainer
Powerplant: One 96.9kW (130hp) de Havilland Gipsy Major I piston engine
Span: 10.31m (33ft 10in)
Length: 7.69m (25ft 3in)
Maximum speed: 233km/h (145mph)
First aircraft flown: 1937
History: The Hawk Trainer was an improved version of the Hawk Major which first appeared in 1937 to meet Air Ministry Specification T40/36. The RAF required a new low-wing monoplane trainer and had evaluated the Miles M2W/X in 1936. The first M14 Magister (L5913) that featured a wider track undercarriage, shorter span wings and a revised rudder shape was delivered to the CFS in September 1937. The Magister was faster than the equivalent biplane trainer, yet offered a modest landing speed of 68km/h (42mph). It was certified for aerobatics and introduced pilots to trailing edge split flaps. By 1941 a total of 1,293 had been built. After the war many Magisters were sold to the civil market where they were certified as Hawk Trainer IIIs.
Survivors: There are three restored Hawk Trainers currently airworthy in the UK — all of them painted as RAF Magisters, including the aircraft operated by the Shuttleworth Collection at Old Warden.
Recognition: Low-wing monoplane with straight leading edges to wings and rounded tips. Oblong tailplane set high on rear fuselage. Narrow top to fin and rudder. Fixed taildragger undercarriage. Two open cockpits, each with small windshields. Usually a polished engine cowling. Small anti-spin strakes forward of tailplane.

Above: Former record-breaking Miles M65 Gemini 1A G-AKKB is displayed by owner James Buckingham. **PRM**

Miles M65 Gemini

Twin-engined light cabin monoplane
Powerplant: Two 74.6kW (100hp) Blackburn Cirrus Minor II piston engines
Span: 11.02m (36ft 2in)
Length: 6.78m (22ft 3in)
Maximum speed: 277km/h (172mph)
First aircraft flown: 26 October 1945
History: A logical development of the Messenger, the twin-engined Gemini was first flown from Woodley soon after the end of World War 2. The prototype Gemini 1 G-AGUS had a fixed undercarriage while the production 1As had rearward-retracting main wheels. Some 140 Geminis were built at Woodley before the company failed at the end of 1947, most of these being sold abroad. The Gemini 3 had DH Gipsy Major 10s. The Gemini 8 had 155hp (115.5kW) Cirrus Major IIIs. Geminis were used by several owners for air racing, the most famous being Fred Dunkerley with his 1A with a cut-down cabin G-AKKB.
Survivors: There are 10 surviving Geminis in the UK, of which only two are currently airworthy. This includes the former racer G-AKKB, owned by James Buckingham at Felton, near Bristol.
Recognition: Twin-engined monoplane with low-set constant chord wings with rounded tips. Underslung engines and protruding flaps on trailing edge of the wing. Spinners in line with nose. Large rounded glazed canopy. Oval shape twin fins and rudders. Main wheels retract rearwards into nacelles.

Below: This privately owned Gemini IA is being restored to fly again, in Essex. **PRM**

Above: *This Morane-Saulnier MS230 has been privately owned at Wycombe Air Park for 27 years.* ***PRM***

Above: *Morane-Saulnier MS230 based at La Ferté Alais in France.* ***APM***

Morane-Saulnier MS230

Single-engined advanced trainer
Powerplant: One 186.4kW (250hp) Salmson 9Ab radial engine
Span: 10.72m (35ft 2in)
Length: 6.93m (22ft 9in)
Maximum speed: 204km/h (127mph)
First aircraft flown: February 1929
History: Designed to meet a 1928 French Air Ministry requirement for a basic training aircraft with advanced performance. Because of its excellent flying and aerobatic qualities more than 1,000 were built. It was used by the *Armée de l'Air* as an observation, gunnery and advanced pilot training aircraft. The larger, but lighter, MS315 that was first flown in 1932 then became the primary trainer. A number served with French naval aviation. All but 77 were built by the parent company; 59 were constructed prewar by SFAN and 18 postwar by Levasseur. MS230s were also privately owned, operated by flying schools and they were also exported to Belgium, Brazil, Greece and Romania.
Survivors: A number of MS230s and 315s remain active in France, Belgium and Switzerland. In the UK the MS230 G-AVEB has been privately owned at Wycombe Air Park for 27 years.
Recognition: Parasol-wing two-seat single-engined aircraft. Large round fuselage with radial engine featuring exposed cylinders. V-bracing to the wing which joins the fuselage with the tops of both struts at the main undercarriage leg. Twin open cockpits, each with small windshield. Curved leading edge and straight trailing edge to fin on rudder. Braced tailplane set high on rear fuselage.

North American AT-6 Texan/Harvard

Single-engined advanced trainer

Powerplant: One 410kW (550hp) Pratt & Whitney Wasp R-1340-AN-1 radial engine

Span: 12.8m (42ft 0.25in)

Length: 8.99m (29ft 6in)

Maximum speed: 341km/h (212mph)

First aircraft flown: April 1936

History: The first prototype of the North American NA-16, built as a basic combat trainer for the US Army Air Corps, was first flown in 1936 and was followed by a first batch of 42 aircraft. Production aircraft for the US services and for export to many countries were built under a wide range of NA, NJ, BC and BT designations. The AT-6C (SNJ-4 and Harvard IIA) differed in being designed to eliminate the use of aluminium-alloy and high-alloy steels. Over 5,000 Harvards eventually saw service with the RAF and Commonwealth air forces, most of which were the MkII with clipped wing tips and a more triangular-shaped fin and rudder. Many of the RAF's Harvards were built by the main sub contractor Noorduyn in Canada.

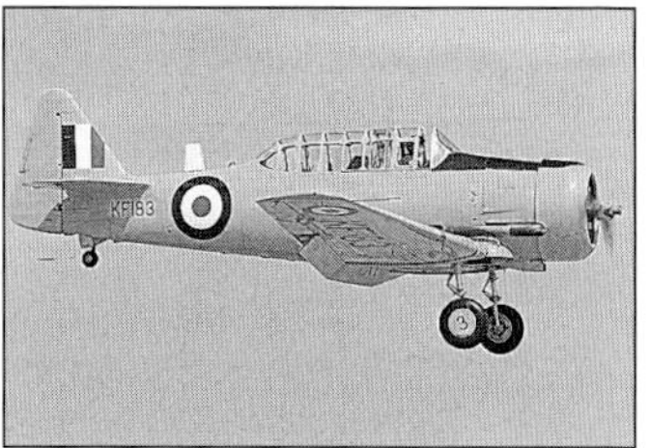

Top: *One of many North American AT-6 Texans flying in former military colours in the USA.* ***PRM***

Above: *North American Harvard IIB, one of two still operated by the DRA at Boscombe Down.* ***PRM***

Survivors: A large number of the 10,000 AT-6s and Harvards built survive around the world. Many aircraft are maintained in flying condition. Some have been modified for racing and others have formed the basis for replicas of other types of aircraft such as the Japanese Zero.

Recognition: Low-wing monoplane with slightly swept leading edge and straight trailing edge. Narrow fuselage with large radial engine. Tandem cockpits with individually-operated sliding enclosures. Pointed fin and rudder. Tailplane set high on rear fuselage. Inward-retracting undercarriage and fixed tailwheel.

North American B-25 Mitchell

Top: North American B-25D Mitchell II based at Duxford with The Fighter Collection. **DJM**

Above: One of more than 30 Mitchells still flying in the USA. **PRM**

Twin-engined medium bomber

Powerplant: Two 1,378kW (1,850hp) Wright R-2600-29 Cyclone 14-cylinder radial engines

Span: 20.6m (67ft 7in)

Length: 16.1m (52ft 11in)

Maximum speed: 455km/h (282mph)

First aircraft flown: 19 August 1940

History: Designed as a high-speed medium bomber in 1939, the B-25 was developed from the NA40 attack bomber. It was built in larger numbers than any other American twin-engined bomber. After an initial interest from the RAF in the B-25B, the improved B-25C was delivered in quantity from mid-1942 as the Mitchell II. It entered RAF service with No 2 Group Bomber Command at West Raynham in September 1942. A total of over 800 were supplied to the RAF under Lend-Lease, the final 300 being Mitchell IIIs (B-25J) — the biggest production version that had a glazed nose and could carry a bomb load of 1,814kg (4,000lb). The last B-25 delivery in August 1945 brought the total produced to 9,816. Several air forces in South America and the Far East used B-25Js for the next 15 years as front-line aircraft.

Survivors: A total of 135 B-25s are known to survive around the world, of which 40 are either in flying condition or under restoration to fly. The majority of these are based in North America, but there are two airworthy examples in Europe with The Fighter Collection at Duxford and The Duke of Brabant Air Force in The Netherlands.

Recognition: Inverted 'gull-wing', mid-set, with marked anhedral outboard of the underslung powerplants. Engine nacelles extend beyond trailing edge of wing. Wings of equal taper with rounded tips. Narrow fuselage, usually with glazed nose. Side-by-side glazed cockpit. Dorsal turret immediately aft of cockpit and a gun position at extreme rear. Twin rectangular fins and rudders. High set tailplane. Tricycle undercarriage, with all wheels fully retractable.

North American F-86 Sabre

Single-seat, single-jet-engined fighter
Data for F-86F
Powerplant: One 26.56kN (5,970lb st) General Electric J47-GE-27 turbojet
Span: 11.30m (37ft 1in)
Length: 11.43m (37ft 6in)
Maximum speed: 1,113km/h (690mph)
First aircraft flown: 1 October 1947
History: The Sabre was originally planned as a conventional aircraft but was delayed for a year to take advantage of German research into swept wings and tails. A 35° sweep angle was adopted. It was the first US fighter to exceed Mach 1 (the speed of sound) in a shallow dive. The production F-86A first flew on 20 May 1948. A 'flying tail' was introduced on the F-86E and this version flew in the Korean War. A total of 1,815 Sabres were built in Canada by Canadair, of which 430 were supplied to the RAF as an interim fighter pending delivery of the Hawker Hunter in 1952-53. The radar-equipped F-86K was produced for NATO air forces. The ultimate USAF version was a completely redesigned F-86H tactical attack fighter. On 19 November 1952 an F-86D established a world air speed record of 698.50mph and this was increased in the following July to 715.69mph. The RF-86 was the high-speed reconnaissance version. The final version was retired by the Air National Guard in 1976.

Top: *North American F-86A Sabre owned by the Golden Apple Trust and operated by the Old Flying Machine Company at Duxford.* ***PRM***

Above: *A former Royal Canadian Air Force F-86E Sabre restored for airshow flying in the USA.* ***PRM***

Survivors: There are about 40 surviving civilian-owned Sabres, of which 33 are located in the USA and four in Australia. The veteran F-86A Sabre G-SABR, owned by the Golden Apple Trust, is operated by The Old Flying Machine Company of Duxford.
Recognition: Low-set swept wings of equal taper. Swept dihedralled tailplane set at extreme rear of fuselage, over jet pipe. Swept fin and rudder with small dorsal fillet at front base of fin. Oval fuselage. Cockpit set forward of leading edge of wing. Visible gun ports in side of nose. Retractable air brakes set in lower fuselage to rear of wing. Pronounced upper lip to nose intake. Often carries twin underwing fuel tanks.

North American P-51 Mustang

Single-engined, single-seat fighter
Data for P-51D
Powerplant: One 1,111kW (1,490hp) Packard Merlin (licence-built R-R Merlin 61 series V-1650-7) V-12 liquid-cooled engine
Span: 11.29m (37ft 0.5in)
Length: 9.81m (32ft 2.5in)
Maximum speed: 703km/h (437mph)
First aircraft flown: 26 October 1940
History: The prototype XP-51 was powered by an 857.5kW (1,150hp) Allison V-1710 engine. It had been designed to an RAF specification for a single-seat fighter. The initial Mustang I/IIs were disappointing in performance, as their engines lost power at medium and high altitudes, so they were solely used for fighter-reconnaissance and Army co-operation. After the trial installation of a Rolls-Royce Merlin, subsequent aircraft were powered by an American-built Packard Merlin. This resulted in the P-51B, P-51C (Mustang III) and tear-drop canopy P-51D (Mustang IV). Total production was 15,586. Mustangs served mainly in Europe, escorting long-range bombing missions from British bases to targets deep in Germany. Production recommenced in 1967 when the Cavalier Aircraft Corp was given a contract for the two-seat F-51D and TF-51D.
Survivors: There are about 300 surviving Mustangs, of which more than half are currently flyable and another 30 or so are under restoration. Most of the P-51s are to be found in the USA, but there is a growing number of airworthy examples in the UK, France, Scandinavia, The Netherlands, Australia and New Zealand. The majority of preserved Mustangs are P-51Ds, including Cavalier-built aircraft, but there are also representative examples of the A-36A, P-51A, P-51C and P-51K/F-6K.
Recognition: Low-wing monoplane with NACA laminar-flow wing section. Wings roughly of equal taper with square tips. Oval-section fuselage. Moulded 'blister' type sliding cockpit cover (on later models) over centre of wing. Coolant and oil radiators in scoop under the fuselage aft of cockpit. Angular fin and rudder, with square tip. Late models have a dorsal extension. Tailplane, of equal taper and square tips, set high on fuselage.

Top: *P-51D Mustang* Gunfighter *is operated by the Confederate Air Force in the USA.* ***APM***

Above: *North American P-51D Mustang* Candyman *owned and operated by The Fighter Collection at Duxford.* ***PRM***

Above: *A restored North American T-28C Trojan shows its stalky undercarriage and long cockpit canopy.* ***PRM***

North American T-28 Trojan

Single-engined basic trainer
Powerplant: One 596.6kW (800hp) Wright R-1300-1 radial engine
Span: 12.22m (40ft 1in)
Length: 9.75m (32ft 0in)
Maximum speed: 456.5km/h (283mph)
First aircraft flown: 26 September 1949
History: The North American NA-159 won the competition for a replacement for the T-6 Texan, that combined primary and basic training characteristics in a single aircraft. It was ordered in quantity in 1950 and 1,194 T-28As were built between 1950 and 1953. The T-28A had provision to carry bombs or rockets under the wings and two 0.50in machine guns. It served at Air Training Command primary flight schools for many years until replaced by the Cessna T-37 in April 1961. The T-28B/C, with a 1,062.6kW (1,425hp) R-1820-86 engine was supplied to the US Navy and the T-28D was developed in 1962 as an armed counter-insurgency aircraft.
Survivors: Numerous examples of all variants of the T-28 remain airworthy in the USA, mostly in the hands of warbird enthusiasts. There are very few to be found outside North America.
Recognition: Low-wing monoplane with straight leading edge, square tips and tapered trailing edge. Small wing fillet at front wing root. Deep short fuselage with large glazed canopy for two crew in tandem. Front cockpit ahead of leading edge of wing. Angular tall fin and rudder, with square top and a pronounced dorsal fillet at front base. Tailplane set on top of rear fuselage. Three-blade 'paddle' propeller with no spinner. Tall, retractable tricycle undercarriage.

Below: *Still wearing its former USN paintwork, this privately owned T-28C Trojan is based in Florida.* ***PRM***

Percival Gull/Vega Gull/Proctor

Single-engined liaison, training and communications aircraft
Data for Proctor IV

Powerplant: One 155.1kW (208hp) de Havilland Gipsy Queen II six-cylinder inverted air-cooled engine
Span: 12.03m (39ft 6in) ***Length:*** 8.58m (28ft 2in) ***Maximum speed:*** 253km/h (157mph)
First aircraft flown: 1932 (Gull); November 1936 (Vega Gull); 8 October 1939 (Proctor)

History: The four-seat Vega Gull light cabin monoplane was developed from the three-seat Gull of the early 1930s, both being designed by Edgar W. Percival. The Proctor, which was externally similar, was chosen by the RAF and Royal Navy for use as a liaison, training and communications aircraft. The Proctor I was a communications type used by the RAF and ATA with side-by-side seats and dual controls. The RN received the Proctor IA as a radio and navigation trainer; the Proctor II and IIA were RAF and RN radio and navigational trainers respectively. The Proctor III was also a radio trainer. Built from 1943, the Proctor IV was a radio trainer for the RAF and had a redesigned fuselage. The last variant to be manufactured was the Proctor V, a postwar civil version, of which 150 were built.

Survivors: Being of all-wood construction there are not many surviving Gulls, Vega Gulls and Proctors. The only airworthy Gull is G-ADPR now in New Zealand, having been sold by the Shuttleworth Collection. Likewise there is only one Vega Gull (G-AEZJ), that is based at White Waltham. Of the dozen or so Proctors known to exist, only three are flyable at present, two of which are based at Biggin Hill.

Recognition: Low wings with a rectangular centre-section and tapering outer sections. Faired and spatted main wheel undercarriage. Large, rounded, glazed cockpit canopy. Rounded fin and rudder. Unbraced tailplane set high on the slab-sided fuselage, ahead of rudder.

Top: *The last airworthy Percival Vega Gull is privately owned at White Waltham.* ***PRM***

Right: *Retaining its original RAF markings, this Percival Proctor IV is flown by its owner from Biggin Hill.* ***DJM***

Percival Prentice

Above: *One of four flyable Percival Prentice T1s which is based at Nayland.* ***PRM***

Single-engined basic trainer
Powerplant: One 187kW (251hp) de Havilland Gipsy Queen 32 six-cylinder, inverted air-cooled engine
Span: 14.02m (46ft 0in)
Length: 9.60m (31ft 6.5in)
Maximum speed: 230 km/h (143mph)
First aircraft flown: 31 March 1946
History: Designed in 1944 to meet Air Ministry Specification T23/44 for a basic trainer to replace the Tiger Moth, the prototype three-seat Prentice T1 was first flown from Luton. A number of modifications were needed to improve handling before a pre-production batch of 20 aircraft was ordered in 1946. First deliveries were made to the CFS in November 1947 and to the RAF College and other Flying Training Schools in 1948. It served until 1955, when it was replaced by Provosts. When released for sale most of the ex-RAF Prentices were purchased by Aviation Traders at Southend. However, conversion to civilian use proved a bigger problem than first anticipated and only a small number were modified between 1956 and 1960.
Survivors: Of the 16 surviving Prentices only four are potentially airworthy at present, including one that has been returned to its former military configuration.
Recognition: Low-wing monoplane with distinctive upturned wing tips. Faired and spatted main wheel undercarriage. Large 'greenhouse' type glazed cockpit for three occupants. Rounded fin and rudder. Tailplane set high on rear fuselage, ahead of rudder.

Piper J-3 Cub

Above: *This privately owned Piper J-3C-65 Cub is painted in wartime USAAC colours.* ***PRM***

Single-engined, two-seat light aircraft
Powerplant: One 48.5-kW (65hp) Continental A65 four-cylinder, horizontally opposed air-cooled engine
Span: 10.73m (35ft 2.5in)
Length: 6.82m (22ft 4.5in)
Maximum speed: 139km/h (87mph)
First aircraft flown: 1938
History: Originated by the Taylor Aircraft Company in 1935, the J-2 Cub, a light, two-seat, high-wing monoplane, was an instant success. Within two years over 750 had been sold. The J-3C Cub, produced by the renamed Piper Aircraft Corporation, appeared in 1938 and remained in production for the next 11 years. Nearly 10,000 had been completed up to the end of 1943, of which 5,673 were the L-4 Grasshopper version for air observation, battlefield communications and training. Postwar many L-4s were sold to civilian owners, joining 14,125 civil Cubs of

various types built between 1938 and 1949. Derivatives of the J-3C include the J-4A Cub Coupé, J-5A Cub Cruiser, PA-12 Super Cruiser, PA-15/17 Vagabond, PA-16 Clipper, PA-18 Super Cub, PA-20 Pacer and the PA-22 Tri-Pacer family.

Survivors: It is not surprising that very many examples of the successful Piper Cub family should remain active in almost every Western country. In Britain there are three prewar J-2 Cubs airworthy and at least six examples of all the other marques. A large number of J-3C Cubs have been painted in USAAC markings as L-4s and similarly there are PA-18 Super Cubs wearing USAAF colours as L-18s.

Recognition: High-wing monoplane with equal-chord wings and rounded tips. V-shaped bracing struts attached to the lower fuselage. Enclosed cabin seating two in tandem, with dual controls. Exposed cylinder heads on either side of nose, with stub exhausts. Elliptical unbraced tailplane. Divided landing gear comprising two side Vs and two half-axles, hinged to cabane below the fuselage. Rounded fin and rudder.

Republic P-47 Thunderbolt

Single-engined, single-seat escort fighter

Data for P-47D

Powerplant: One 1,890.4kW (2,535hp) Pratt & Whitney R-2800-59 Double Wasp 18-cylinder two-row radial engine

Span: 12.42m (40ft 9.25in)

Length: 11.03m (36ft 1.25in)

Maximum speed: 690km/h (429mph)

First aircraft flown: 6 May 1941

Above: *Confederate Air Force Republic P-47N Thunderbolt flown by the American Airpower Heritage Flying Museum at Midland, Texas.* ***PRM***

History: The P-47 was designed around the large Double Wasp engine to reflect the needs of the aerial war in Europe, by carrying increased armament and having a greater fuel capacity than contemporary fighters. A large-diameter four-blade propeller was fitted to absorb the high power. The P-47's operational début was in April 1943. The P-47D was supplied to the RAF initially as the Thunderbolt I and subsequently the Thunderbolt II. Early models, with sliding cockpit, were known as 'Razorbacks'. Later D models featured the 'teardrop' cockpit and a dorsal fin. The Thunderbolt became the last radial-engined fighter to serve in quantity with the USAAF. A total of 15,683 Thunderbolts were built. Postwar many served with Air National Guard squadrons until 1955. These aircraft were then sold to several South American air arms.

Survivors: There are 50 surviving P-47s, of which 12 are potentially airworthy and a further four are under active restoration. One composite P-47D/N is operated by The Fighter Collection at Duxford. It is painted in 78th FG/82nd FS, USAAF colour scheme as '22667 No Guts - No Glory'.

Recognition: Low-wing monoplane with elliptical wings and noticeable dihedral. Large radial engine and deep oval-section fuselage. Curved upper and lower fuselage lines tapering to the rear. 'Bubble' cockpit canopy on later models. Curved trailing edge of tailplane and rudder. Large four-blade propeller.

Royal Aircraft Factory SE5A

Single-seat scout fighter

Powerplant: One 149.3kW (200hp) Wolseley W4a Viper V-8 water-cooled piston engine

Span: 8.11m (26ft 7.5in)

Length: 6.38m (20ft 11in)

Maximum speed: 193km/h (120mph)

First aircraft flown: 22 November 1916

History: The SE (Scout Experimental) 5 was designed in 1916 by the Royal Aircraft Factory at Farnborough. Mass-production was embarked upon by the Austin Motor Co, Martinsyde Ltd, Air Navigation and Engineering Co, Vickers Ltd and Wolseley Motors. Many of the Allied aces gained their victories on the SE5A. Some 5,000 were built in Britain for the RFC and American Expeditionary Force. The SE5A proved to be an excellent fighter and helped the RAF to gain air supremacy over the Western Front in 1918. Many SE5s were sold after the war ended, some to overseas air arms and others to civil operators in the UK.

Survivors: One airworthy RAF SE5A survives in the UK with the Shuttleworth Collection at Old Warden and an SE5E is with Kermit Weeks flying museum at Polk City, Florida.

Recognition: Single-bay biplane with staggered, constant chord wings of equal length. Lewis gun on Foster mount on upper wing. Exposed engine manifolds on each side of nose. Propeller shaft mounted low on wide nose that incorporates the coolant radiator. Open cockpit, with small windshield, in line with lower trailing edge. Fairing behind cockpit. Sloping leading edge and straight trailing edge to the fin and rudder. Small ventral fin under braced tailplane. Slender struts to fixed undercarriage.

Above: *The UK's only airworthy original Royal Aircraft Factory SE5A is based at Old Warden.* ***PRM***

Below: *This restored Royal Aircraft Factory SE5E flies in the USA.* ***PRM***

Above: *Ryan PT-22 operated by the PT Flight based at Cosford.* ***PRM***

Ryan PT-22 Recruit

Single-engined, two-seat primary trainer
Powerplant: One 119.3kW (160hp) Kinner R-540-1 five-cylinder air-cooled radial engine
Span: 9.14m (30ft 0in)
Length: 6.55m (21ft 6in)
Maximum speed: 206.5km/h (128mph)
First aircraft flown: 3 February 1939 (XPT-16 prototype)
History: With the huge expansion of the US Army and Navy air forces in 1940/41 Ryan was one of three manufacturers to produce primary and basic trainers. This was the first monoplane trainer as, until 1939, all Army primary trainers had been biplanes. The first version was the PT-16, an all-metal aircraft, a militarised version of the Ryan S-T. During 1941 the Menasco Vee in-line engine was discarded by the Army in favour of the Kinner R-440 radial. The PT-20 and PT-21 differed by engine type. The more powerful Kinner engine fitted to the PT-22, known as the Recruit, was without wheel spats. 1,023 were delivered by 1942 when production ended.
Survivors: There are many surviving airworthy Ryan PTs in the USA, most retaining their former military paint schemes. There are five PT-21/22s active in the UK, all of which carry USAAC markings.
Recognition: Low-wing monoplane with external wire bracing to the top of the fuselage and to the main undercarriage legs. Open cockpits in tandem. Streamlined nose fairing with projecting, uncowled cylinders. Wings of equal chord with rounded tips and slight sweep. Elliptical braced tailplane. Curved leading and trailing edge to tail fin. Ungainly fixed taildragger undercarriage.

Above: *A UK-based Ryan PT-22 Recruit.* ***PRM***

Saab-91D Safir

Above: This privately owned Saab 91D Safir is one of four registered in the UK. ***PRM***

Below: Saab 91D/2 Safir owned by Sylmar Aviation at Aldermaston. ***PRM***

Single-engined four-seat cabin monoplane
Powerplant: One 134kW (180hp) Lycoming 0-350-A1A piston engine
Span: 10.59m (34ft 9in)
Length: 9.16m (26ft 4in)
Maximum speed: 266.14km/h (165mph)
First aircraft flown: 20 November 1945

History: The initial production series, the Saab-91A, was powered by a 108kW (145hp) de Havilland Gypsy Major X engine, and 17 were delivered to the Imperial Ethiopian Air Force as primary trainers. Re-engined with a Lycoming as the Saab-91B, the Safir was introduced as the Swedish Air Force's standard trainer (Sk50). Original models were three-seaters but the -91C and -91D were four seaters. Some 320 Safirs were sold to 20 countries, including use as executive transports, military trainers and for airline pilot training, with Lufthansa and Sabena being the main users in this category.

Survivors: Over 50 Safirs remain in existence, more than half of which are airworthy. This includes two in the UK (G-BCFW and G-HRLK).

Recognition: Low-wing monoplane with a long slim fuselage. Large glazed cockpit with pilot sitting ahead of leading edge of wing. Large rectangular windows for rear passengers. Wings of equal taper with square tips. Near-vertical leading edge to fin and rudder. Retractable tricycle undercarriage, main wheels retracting inwards into fuselage sides.

Above: *Replica Sopwith F1 Camel that flies with the Blue Max Movie Museum at Wycombe Air Park.* ***PRM***

Sopwith F1 Camel

Single-engined, single-seat biplane fighter
Powerplant: One 96.9kW (130hp) Clerget 9B nine-cylinder rotary engine
Span: 8.53m (28ft 0in)
Length: 5.72m (18ft 9in)
Maximum speed: 182km/h (113mph)
First aircraft flown: 22 December 1916
History: The Sopwith F1 was designed by Herbert Smith in 1916 and built as a scout fighter for the RFC and as a ship-based fighter for the RNAS. It was fitted with two Vickers machine guns, synchronised to fire through the propeller. The partial fairing over the guns gave the F1 a humped appearance, hence the nickname Camel that was later adopted officially. First deliveries were made to the RFC in June 1917 and the new type entered service with No 70 Squadron. In action the fighter destroyed at least 1,294 enemy aircraft during World War 1, a greater total than any other contemporary fighter aircraft. Nearly 5,500 Camels were produced, of which only 340 were the naval 2F1 version. By the Armistice Camels equipped 32 RAF squadrons. Later production Camels were fitted with the 118.1kW (150hp) Bentley BR1 rotary engine.
Survivors: Only six, complete, original Camels are believed to exist (four F1s and two 2F1s) and all but one of these are displayed in museums. The only airworthy Camel is B6291 that was restored by AJD Engineering and sold to the USA in 1993. There are a number of replicas, built to original drawings, flying in the UK and USA.
Recognition: Single-bay biplane with staggered wings of equal length. Very short nose and humped-back appearance. Single open cockpit under trailing edge of upper wing. Long V-struts to undercarriage, with a cross-axle between relatively large wheels with hub-caps. Small, rounded fin and rudder, the latter being aft of the fuselage and tail skid. Bracing wires from the tailplane to the fin. Vickers machine guns mounted on upper cowling synchronised to fire between the propeller blades.

Above: The Shuttleworth Collection's airworthy Sopwith Pup, based at Old Warden. ***PRM***

Sopwith Pup

Single-engined, single-seat biplane fighter
Powerplant: One 59.6kW (80hp) Le Rhône 9C nine-cylinder rotary engine
Span: 8.08m (26ft 6in)
Length: 5.89m (19ft 3.75in)
Maximum speed: 179km/h (111mph)
First aircraft flown: February 1916
History: The Pup was a development of the Sopwith 1½ Strutter, being a scaled-down version, with a low-wing loading, to give better performance at higher levels. It entered service with the RNAS in September 1916. For the following 12 months it was able to acquit itself well against the best German opposition over the Western Front with both the RNAS and RFC. In August 1917 a Pup made the first landing on a Navy vessel under way at sea. In June 1917 it made the first take-off from the gun platform of HMS *Yarmouth*. The Pup also conducted pioneer experiments using arrester gear. Sopwith built 170 Pups for the RNAS, while other firms built 1,670 for the RFC, many being assigned to Home Defence units. A small number were converted after the war for civilian use, as the Sopwith Dove.
Survivors: There are two (part) original Sopwith Pups in flyable condition. The Museum of Army Flying at Middle Wallop has Desmond St Cyrien's rebuilt Pup (N5195) and the Shuttleworth Collection has a converted Sopwith Dove (G-EBKY/N6181) in its airworthy fleet. There are also two flying replicas being built.
Recognition: Single-bay biplane with staggered wings of equal span. Very short nose with broad, fully-cowled rotary engine. Straight deck upper fuselage with single-seat open cockpit situated under leading edge of upper wing. Curved fin and rudder. One Vickers machine gun on upper engine cowling. V-struts to undercarriage main wheels.

Sopwith Triplane

Single-engined, single-seat triplane fighter
Powerplant: One 96.9kW (130hp) Clerget 9B nine-cylinder rotary engine
Span: 8.08m (26ft 6in)
Length: 5.74m (18ft 10in)
Maximum speed: 182km/h (113mph)
First aircraft flown: 28 May 1916
History: The Triplane was designed as a replacement for the Pup with a better rate of climb and manoeuvrability. When introduced by the RNAS in February 1917 the new Triplane could outclimb everything else in the sky. The Germans were very concerned and instructed Fokker to build a triplane (Dr1) for them. As the RFC was then receiving SPADs, production Sopwith Triplanes went to the RNAS. It was very successful between April and October 1917, but delivery of the yet better Camel stopped the Triplane and only 140 were delivered, the last on 19 October 1917.
Survivors: Two original Sopwith Triplanes survive — both in museums (RAF Museum, Hendon and the Monino Museum, Moscow). There are two flying replicas — one at Old Warden with the Shuttleworth Collection (G-BOCK/N6290) and the other privately owned at Dunkeswell (G-PENY/5492).
Recognition: Single-bay triplane with three slender wings of equal length, the mid-plane resting on the top of the fuselage. Single-seat open cockpit, immediately behind trailing edge of centre wing. Straight deck to upper fuselage and curved lower fuselage. Cowled rotary engine. Small curved fin and rudder and a braced tailplane.

Below: *Replica Sopwith Triplane in RNAS markings is operated by The Shuttleworth Collection.* ***PRM***

Stampe SV4A/B/C

Single-engined, two-seat biplane trainer
Data for SV4A

Powerplant: One 97kW (130hp) de Havilland Gipsy Major II engine
Span: 8.38m (27ft 6in)
Length: 6.96m (22ft 10in)
Maximum speed: 180km/h (112mph)
First aircraft flown: May 1933
History: The SV4 two-seat primary training biplane was first introduced in the early 1930s by the Stampe-et-Vertongen company in Belgium. A contemporary of the Tiger Moth, it did not get the same prod-uction opportunity until after the war. A number of SV4B trainers were built by Société Stampe et Rénard for the Belgian Air Force. Some 1,000 were produced under licence in France as the SV4C with the 104.3kW (140hp) Renault 4 Pei engine. In the 1950s and 1960s most of the French and Belgian Air Force SV4s were sold to civilian customers. The SV4D was produced mainly for glider towing and was fitted with a 123kW (165hp) Rolls-Royce Continental IO-360-A engine.
Survivors: A popular vintage aircraft across Europe, there are many airworthy examples, including more than 40 in the UK. Some have been converted to Lycoming or Continental power.
Recognition: Single-engined biplane with slightly swept lower and upper wings of equal length. Rounded tips with ailerons on both wings. Fixed taildragger undercarriage with cross bracing on struts. Rounded fin, rudder and tailplane, with cut-out at base. Twin open cockpits.

Above: *SNCAN Stampe SV-4C, with Gipsy Major 1C engine, is based at Redhill.* ***PRM***

Above:
One of over 200 Stampes still active in Britain, France and Belgium. ***PRM***

Supermarine Spitfire

Above: Supermarine Spitfire Vb flown by the Battle of Britain Memorial Flight at RAF Coningsby. ***PRM***

Single-engined, single-seat fighter
Data for Spitfire Vb
Powerplant: One 1,073.8kW (1,440hp) Rolls-Royce Merlin 45 V-12 liquid-cooled engine (MkV)
Span: 11.23m (36ft 10in); clipped wing 9.93m (32ft 7in)
Length: 9.12m (29ft 11in)
Maximum speed: 603km/h (374mph) ***First aircraft flown:*** 5 March 1936
History: The Spitfire dates back to the Schneider Trophy-winning Supermarine S6B of 1931. Designed by R. J. Mitchell, the Spitfire prototype (K5054) was built to Specification F37/34 and was powered by a Rolls-Royce V-12, later named the Merlin. It was soon ordered into production and initial deliveries were made to the RAF in July 1938, being the first British all-metal stressed-skin fighter. By September 1939 the RAF had nine squadrons of Spitfires and orders placed for 4,000 aircraft. Successive marks of Spitfire had improved Merlin engines and the Griffon was introduced on the MkXIV. The Spitfire V was the major variant of the middle war years with 6,479 built. The final versions of the fighter were the Mks22 and strengthened 24, bringing the total number of Spitfires built to over 20,000. The last RAF front-line flight was made by a Spitfire XIX of No 81 Sqn in Malaya on 1 April 1954.
Survivors: At the end of 1995 there were 48 flyable Spitfires from a total of over 180 known to be in existence. A further 45 were actively being restored at this date. Of the airworthy examples, nearly half are based in the UK, covering most versions (except the Seafire), with the Battle of Britain Memorial Flight operating a MkIIa, Vb and two PRXIXs. Most of the civilian-owned aircraft are based at Duxford, with The Fighter Collection and The Old Flying Machine Company.
Recognition: Low-wing monoplane. The standard wings for medium-level fighter versions were elliptical in plan; shorter-span wings with squared tips were fitted to the 'LF' variants for low-level operations, and extended-span wings with pointed tips were fitted to the high flying photo-reconnaissance Spitfires. Oval-shaped fuselage. Enclosed cockpit over wing with a sliding canopy and hinged panel in port side of fuselage for entry or exit. Narrow track undercarriage — main wheels retracting outwards into wings. Rounded fin and rudder (on most versions). Rounded tailplane set on top of rear fuselage with cut-outs to allow rudder movement.

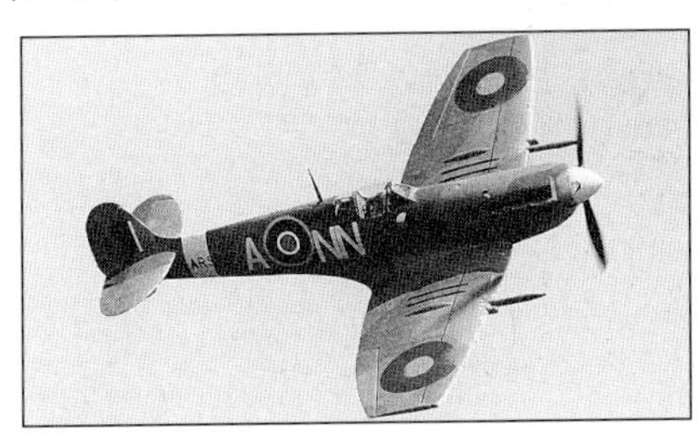

Above: Clipped-wing Spitfire LFVc that has been with The Shuttleworth Collection for many years and regularly flown at Old Warden. ***APM***

Above: *This Confederate Air Force Vought FG-1D Corsair flies with the American Airpower Heritage Flying Museum at Midland, Texas.* ***PRM***

Vought F4U Corsair

Single-seat, carrier-based fighter-bomber
Data for F4U-1 Corsair
Powerplant: One 1,677kW (2,250hp) Pratt & Whitney Double Wasp R-2800-8 18-cylinder two-row air-cooled radial engine
Span: 12.49m (41ft 0in)
Length: 10.16m (33ft 4in)
Maximum speed: 669km/h (415mph)
First aircraft flown: 29 May 1940
History: The XF4U-1 was designed prewar and first flown in May 1940. Deliveries commenced on 3 October 1942 and it served with the US Navy and Marine Corps from early 1943. Under Lend-Lease over 2,000 Corsairs were supplied to the Fleet Air Arm, serving from 1943 to August 1946 with 19 FAA squadrons operating from carriers, mainly in the Far East. Goodyear produced over 4,000 Corsairs under the designation FG-1, all having the raised cockpit canopy. The last of 12,571 Corsairs came off the production line in December 1952.
Survivors: Of nearly 90 surviving Corsairs a surprising 35 are potentially flyable, with another 20 on rebuild to fly again. Most of these are located in North America where they are popular for air racing and displays. There are two in the UK (at Duxford) with others operating in France, Austria and Scandinavia.
Recognition: Low-wing monoplane with inverted 'gull' inner section and marked dihedral on the outer wing. Main wheels retract backwards into the underside of the wings and enclosed by hinged doors. Large radial engine and four-blade propeller with no spinner. Cockpit set well back in line with the wing trailing edge; high-back rear fuselage. Tall fin and rudder, with rounded top, set ahead of angular tailplane. Long tailwheel that retracts inside the tail cone and covered by hinged doors.

Left: *Currently the only airworthy Corsair in the UK, this FG-1D painted in RNZAF markings is operated by The Old Flying Machine Company at Duxford.* ***DJM***

Vultee BT-13/15 Valiant

Above: The sole Vultee BT-15 Valiant in the UK is operated by the PT Flight based at RAF Cosford. ***PRM***

Single-engined, two-seat basic trainer
Powerplant: One 335kW (450hp) Pratt & Whitney R-985-AN-1 Wasp Junior radial engine
Span: 12.80m (42ft 0in)
Length: 8.78m (28ft 10in)
Maximum speed: 290.3km/h (180mph)
First aircraft flown: 24 March 1939 (BT-13)
History: The BT-13 (known as the Vibrator) powered by a 335kW (450hp) Pratt & Whitney R-985-AN-1 Wasp Junior engine and BT-15 Valiant with the similar power Wright R-975-11 engine were produced from 1940 to 1944, and served as the basic type for all aircrew trained in the US during the period. The build-up of Valiant production was so rapid that engine production could not cope, so most were produced as BT-15s. Production ceased in mid-1944 after 11,537 Valiants had been delivered to the USAAF as BT-13s/BT-15s and the US Navy as SNVs. By 1945 the BT-15 was being replaced by more advanced types, such as the AT-6 Texan, and the type was quickly withdrawn from service.
Survivors: Over 100 Valiants, of all three versions, are currently registered and potentially flyable in North America. Nine BT-13s were converted at Long Beach, California, as replica Aichi Vals for the movie Tora! Tora! Tora! in 1968. Most of these are still flying, as are a similar number of Kate replicas that used BT-13 rear sections. There is just one BT-15 (N58566) in the UK, operated by the PT Flight at RAF Cosford.
Recognition: Low-wing monoplane with a straight leading edge, round tips and tapered trailing edge. Small wing root fillet at rear. Large radial engine and two-blade propeller. Diamond-shaped tailplane set at extremity of rear fuselage, and an angular fin and rudder. 'Greenhouse'-type canopy for crew seated in tandem. Fixed taildragger undercarriage. Small fairing at base of tailwheel.

Above: One of many Vultee BT-15 Valiants still flying in the USA. ***PRM***

Above: *Westland Lysander IIIA, owned by Wessex Aviation & Transport, is operated by the Aircraft Restoration Company at Duxford.* ***PRM***

Westland Lysander

Single-engined, two-seat army co-operation aircraft

Data for Lysander III

Powerplant: One 648kW (870hp) Bristol Mercury XX nine-cylinder radial engine
Span: 15.24m (50ft 0in)
Length: 9.29m (30ft 6in)
Maximum speed: 381km/h (237mph)
First aircraft flown: 15 June 1936

History: The Lysander — affectionately known as the Lizzie — was designed to meet Specification A39/34 as an army co-operation aircraft. The type entered service with No 16 Squadron at Old Sarum in June 1938. Production by Westland continued through to January 1942, by which time 1,325 had been built, of four marks; 325 more were built in Canada, by National Steel Car. Although the Lysander was withdrawn from army co-operation duties in 1942 (replaced by the P-40 Tomahawk) it continued to operate for communications, air-sea rescue, target-towing and special duties. This included flying in and out of enemy-occupied territory to drop spies and evacuate key personnel.

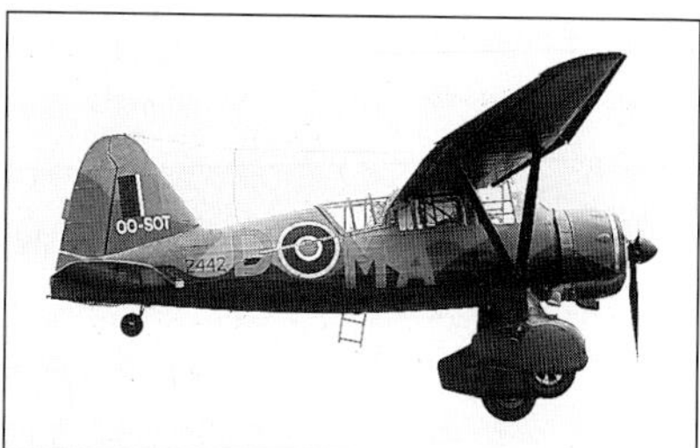

Above: *This Westland Lysander IIIA is based in Belgium but appears at airshows across Europe.* ***PRM***

Survivors: All but one of the 20 surviving Lysanders served with the RCAF. Of these, four are potentially airworthy in Europe (three in the UK, one in Belgium) and three in North America.

Recognition: High-wing monoplane with distinctive tapered shape to its wings. V-strut wing bracing to top of the undercarriage housing. Very long legs, with formed undercarriage and spats. Large radial engine, with deep glazed cockpit behind. Relatively large pointed fin and rudder and low-set tailplane.

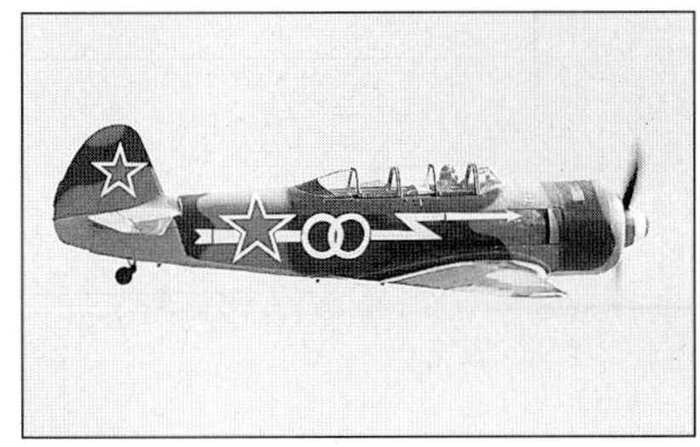

Right: *The Fighter Collection's Czech built Yakovlev C-11s, one of four active in the UK.* ***PRM***

Yakovlev Yak-11

Single-engined, two-seat intermediate trainer

Powerplant: One 425kW (730hp) Shvestov ASL-21 seven-cylinder radial engine
Span: 9.4m (30ft 10in)
Length: 8.5m (27ft 11in)
Maximum speed: 475km/h (295mph)
First aircraft flown: 1946
History: Designed as an advanced combat trainer, the Yak-11 (NATO name Moose) was an offshoot of the long line of Yakovlev fighters of World War 2. Production in the Soviet Union totalled 3,850 and the type was the first to be used by the expanding communist satellite bloc air forces in the 1950s. In 1954 it was put into production in Czechoslovakia as the C-11 and 707 were produced. Replacement of the Yak-11 in the basic trainer role started in 1963, but it continued as an interim advanced trainer prior to the introduction of the L-29 Delfin.
Survivors: Over 100 Yak-11s survive in airworthy condition, mainly in Eastern Europe and the former USSR. There are six Yak-11s currently flyable in the UK, mostly based at Little Gransden and Duxford. Many of the survivors were built by LET in Czechoslovakia.
Recognition: Low-wing monoplane with wings of equal taper and small rounded tips. Main wheels retract inwards into the wings. Deep fuselage and large radial engine, with large spinner. Long, shallow, glazed canopy. Pointed fin and rudder. Tailplane set high on rear fuselage.

Above: *A privately owned SPP/Yakovlev C-11 based at North Weald.* ***PRM***

Above: *Privately owned BA Swallow 2 (Pobjoy Niagara 3) is flown from Old Warden.* **PRM**

BK/BA Swallow

Single-engined, two-seat light aircraft

Powerplant: One 56kW (75hp) British Salmson AD9 (British Klemm) or one 67.1kW (90hp) Pobjoy Cataract III (BA Swallow)

Span: 13.03m (42ft 8.5in)

Length: 7.92m (26ft 0in)

Maximum speed: 180.6km/h (112mph)

First aircraft flown: 1927 (Klemm L25); November 1933 (BK Swallow)

Production & survivors: Originally known as British Klemm, the BA Swallow was a licence-built Klemm L25. A total of 178 Swallows were built by BK/BA and mostly sold to private owners and flying schools. Examples of all three types are potentially airworthy in the UK, including a rare British Klemm L25C that is being restored.

Bell 47G Sioux

Light civil helicopter

Powerplant: One 201.5kW (270hp) Lycoming TVO-435-F1A piston engine

Main rotor diameter: 11.32m (37ft 2in)

Length: 9.63m (31ft 7in)

Maximum speed: 135km/h (84mph)

First aircraft flown: 8 December 1945

Production & survivors: The first Bell 47 was sold on 31 December 1946 and it was the first helicopter to receive a commercial licence. Produced by Bell until 1974 and by Westland and Agusta until 1976, the Sioux served with 30 air arms, including the Army Air Corps. Over 30 are currently airworthy in the UK, including three examples of the 'covered' Bell 47J.

Above: *Westland-Bell 47G-4A, privately owned at Redhill, flies in a US Army Vietnam colour scheme.* **PRM**

Bristol F2B Fighter

Two-seat, single-engined biplane-fighter
Powerplant: One 205kW (275hp) Rolls-Royce Falcon III engine
Span: 11.96m (39ft 3in)
Length: 7.87m (25ft 10in)
Maximum speed: 202km/h (125mph)
First aircraft flown: 9 September 1916
Production & survivors: The Bristol Fighter entered service in February 1917 and it remained on the Bristol lines until September 1919 when the 3,576th Fighter was delivered to the RNZAF. It was finally withdrawn from squadron service in 1932. A grand total of 5,308 Bristol Fighters were built. Today just two Bristol Fighters remain in flying condition in the UK — with the Shuttleworth Collection at Old Warden and the newly restored F2B with The Fighter Collection at Duxford.

Above: *This original Bristol F2B Fighter has been owned by the Shuttleworth Collection for many years.* ***PRM***

Bristol Beaufighter

Twin-engined, two-seat night fighter/torpedo strike fighter
Powerplant: Two 1,294kW (1,735hp) Bristol Hercules XVII radial air-cooled engines
Span: 17.62m (57ft 10in)
Length: 12.69m (41ft 8in)
Maximum speed: 515km/h (320mph)
First aircraft flown: 17 July 1939
Production & survivors: The Beaufighter entered service with the RAF in September 1940. A total of 5,564 were produced in England and 364 in Australia. The type saw its career out as a target tug and the last one in service, RD761, was withdrawn in Singapore in May 1960. Three Beaufighters are being restored to flying condition (two in the UK) from 11, mostly ex-Australian Air Force, surviving airframes.

Above: *The Fighter Collection at Duxford is restoring a Bristol Beaufighter similar to this, to flying condition.* ***PRM***

Bücker Bü 133C Jungmeister

Single-engined, aerobatic biplane
Powerplant: One 119kW (160hp) Siemans Sh 14A-4 radial engine
Span: 6.59m (21ft 7.5in)
Length: 5.89m (19ft 4in)
Maximum speed: 216km/h (134mph)
First aircraft flown: 1935
Production & survivors:
In addition to production (until 1945) by Bücker Flugzeugbau GmbH, the Jungmeister was built by Construcciones Aeronauticas SA in Spain for the Spanish Air Force under the designation ES-1, and 47 were built in Switzerland by the former Dornier-Werke for the Swiss Air Force. It was put back into production in the 1960s as the Bü133F with a 164kW (220hp) Franklin 6A-650-C1 engine. The Jungmeister remains popular for aerobatics and a number of examples are regularly flown in local competitions. There are six currently flyable in the UK.

Above: *Privately owned Bücker Bü 133D Jungmeister painted in Swiss Air Force colours and based at White Waltham.* ***PRM***

De Havilland DH80A Puss Moth

Single-engined, long-range cabin tourer
Powerplant: One 89.5kW (120hp) de Havilland Gipsy Major III engine
Span: 11.20m (36ft 9in)
Length: 7.62m (25ft 0in)
Maximum speed: 205km/h (127mph)
First aircraft flown:
9 September 1929
Production & survivors:
A total of 259 Puss Moths were built, the last being delivered in March 1933 when replaced by the Leopard Moth. A majority of the surviving aircraft were impressed into the RAF in 1940 but less than a dozen survived to return to the civil register in 1946. Today that number has been reduced to just four.

Above: *The unusual main undercarriage leg identifies this as a de Havilland DH80A Puss Moth.* ***PRM***

De Havilland DH85 Leopard Moth

Single-engined, light cabin monoplane
Powerplant: One 96.9kW (130hp) de Havilland Gipsy Major I piston engine
Span: 11.43m (37ft 6in)
Length: 7.47m (24ft 6in)
Maximum speed: 225.8km/h (140mph)
First aircraft flown: 27 May 1933
Production & survivors: The wooden Leopard Moth replaced the welded steel Puss Moth in production. Although lighter and easier to build, only 132 were built, 71 of which were registered in the UK. A number were impressed into military service during the war for communications duties. Currently seven Leopard Moths are active in the UK.

Above: *Dorset-based Leopard Moth in an immaculate black and gold scheme and fitted with wheel spats.* ***DJM***

De Havilland DH88 Comet

Twin-engined racing monoplane
Powerplant: Two 171.5kW (230hp) de Havilland Gipsy Six R piston engines
Span: 13.41m (44ft 0in)
Length: 8.83m (29ft 0in)
Maximum speed: 382km/h (237mph)
First aircraft flown: 8 September 1934
Production & survivors: Designed in 1933 to compete in the England to Australia air race, three Comets were built in 1934 (G-ACSP, 'CSR and 'CSS) and two more the following year (F-ANPZ and G-ADEF). Only the race-winning G-ACSS *Grosvenor House* survives intact. It is in flying condition but currently grounded at Old Warden. Some original parts of G-ACSP are being used for a long-term rebuild project in Gloucestershire, and a replica of G-ACSS is flying in the USA.

Above:
The record-breaking de Havilland DH88 Comet Grosvenor House *is based at Old Warden.* ***PRM***

De Havilland DH90 Dragonfly

Twin-engined, five-seat cabin biplane
Powerplant: Two 96.9kW (130hp) de Havilland Gipsy Major piston engines
Span: 13.11m (43ft 0in)
Length: 9.65m (31ft 8in) 31ft 8in
Maximum speed: 232km/h (144mph)
First aircraft flown: 12 August 1935
Production & survivors: A scaled-down Dragon Rapide in shape but not in structure, two-thirds of the 67 Dragonflies produced were sold abroad and used on feeder lines and for charter flying. Today there are two restored Dragonflies (G-AEDT and 'EDU) operated by de Havilland enthusiasts in the UK.

Above: *De Havilland DH90 Dragonfly privately owned at Rendcomb, Glos.* ***PRM***

De Havilland DH94 Moth Minor

Single-engined, tandem-seat, low-wing monoplane
Powerplant: One 59.5kW (80hp) de Havilland Gipsy Minor piston engine
Span: 11.14m (36ft 7in)
Length: 7.45m (24ft 5in)
Maximum speed: 160.93km/h (100mph)
First aircraft flown: 22 June 1937
Production & survivors: Over 100 of these successors to the Moth biplane family had been built at Hatfield by 1940, when production ceased. It continued to be manufactured in Australia, where the RAAF received over 40.
In England 32 were impressed into service with the RAF during the war. There are only three Moth Minors potentially airworthy in the UK at present.

Above: *The only airworthy DH94 Moth Minor is flown by the Confederate Air Force at Brownsville, Texas.* ***PRM***

Fairey Flycatcher

Single-engined, single-seat, carrier-borne biplane fighter
Powerplant: One 300kW (400hp) Armstrong Siddeley Jaguar III/IV piston engine
Span: 8.84m (29ft 0in)
Length: 7.01m (23ft 0in)
Maximum speed: 214.5km/h (133mph)
First aircraft flown: 28 November 1922
Production & survivors: From 1923 to 1934 the Flycatcher was the only Fleet fighter in the Fleet Air Arm. 192 Flycatchers were produced for the FAA, the last was delivered in June 1930. It was replaced by the Nimrod and Osprey and was declared obsolete in April 1935. G-BEYB is a Flycatcher Replica with a Pratt & Whitney R985 engine registered on 17 July 1977. It is owned by John S. Fairey and is painted in 405 Flt FAA colour scheme as S1287.

Above: *This Fairey Flycatcher replica was built using original plans and is the only existing representative of the type.* ***PRM***

Hawker Sea Hawk

Single-seat, carrier-based fighter-bomber
Data for Sea Hawk FGA 6
Powerplant: One 24.05kN (5,400lb st) Rolls-Royce Nene 103 turbojet
Span: 11.89m (39ft 0in)
Length: 12.08m (39ft 8in)
Maximum speed: 958km/h (599mph)
First aircraft flown: 2 September 1947 (P1040) 3 September 1948 (F1)
Production & survivors: Over 400 Sea Hawks (all but 35 built by Armstrong Whitworth Aircraft) were delivered to the Fleet Air Arm between 1953 and 1956 as replacements for the Attacker and Sea Furies. The F1 first entered service with 806 Squadron at Brawdy in March 1953. Five different variants followed (F2, FB3, FGA4, FB5 and FGA6). The fighter role was taken over by Scimitars in 1960 and the Sea Hawk was relegated to second-line duties. Although there are no Sea Hawks currently flyable, the RN Historic Flight's aircraft is being restored by British Aerospace and another in the USA.

Above: *Hawker Sea Hawk FGA6 owned by the RN Historic Flight is currently being restored to fly again.* ***PRM***

Above: *Operated from Bristol, this Miles Messenger 2A is painted to represent Mony's aircraft (RG333).* ***PRM***

Miles Messenger

Single-engined, four-seat, low-wing cabin monoplane
Powerplant: One 140hp (104.3kW) de Havilland Gipsy Major (Messenger I/4A); 155hp (114.4kW) Blackburn Cirrus Major III (Messenger 2A)
Span: 11.02m (36ft 2in)
Length: 7.32m (24ft 0in)
Maximum speed: 199.55km/h (124mph)
First aircraft flown: 12 September 1942
Production & survivors: The Messenger I was built for the RAF and 21 were delivered for light liaison duties. A total of 64 of the more powerful Messenger 2As were built postwar, including nine for overseas customers. The RAF's fleet was also sold to private owners as the Messenger 4A. There are four Messengers currently flyable in the UK, including one recently restored Mk4B G-AKVZ. One aircraft (G-AIEK) has been converted to represent Monty's Messenger (Mk4 RG333), the first RAF aircraft to land in France after D-Day.

Roe IV Triplane

Single-engined triplane
Powerplant: One 23.32kW (35hp) Green engine
Span: Upper 9.75m (32ft 0in); Bottom 6.09m (20ft 0in)
Length: 9.15m (30ft 0in) — increased to 10.36m (34ft 0in) in February 1911
Maximum speed: 64.37km/h (40mph)
First aircraft flown: September 1910
Production & survivors: In January 1909 A. V. Roe commenced a triplane design using a patent for a novel control system applied to a tandem triplane arrangement. The Roe II followed in March 1910 and the Roe III, a two-seater, the same year. The Roe IV, the last pioneering triplane, emerged late in 1910. It was a single-seater with reduced span, different tail with moving elevators. A Roe Type IV Replica with an AOC Cirrus 3 engine is operated by the Shuttleworth Collection at Old Warden and carries no external marks. The replica was built for the film Those Magnificent Men in Their Flying Machines in the early 1960s.

Above: *This replica Roe IV Triplane flies at Old Warden when weather conditions permit.* ***DJM***

Scottish Aviation Twin Pioneer

Twin-engined, high-wing, light transport aircraft
Powerplant: Two 477.2kW (640hp) Alvis Leonides 531 radial piston engines
Span: 23.3m (76ft 6in)
Length: 15.05m (45ft 3in)
Maximum speed: 266km/h (165mph)
First aircraft flown: 25 June 1955
Production & survivors: Although Scottish Aviation hoped to sell 200 aircraft, only 87 were built. The RAF ordered a batch of 20, entering service with No 78 Squadron in Aden in March 1958. Eventually they received 39 aircraft that served mainly in Bahrain, Aden and Singapore until the type was withdrawn from operational service in 1968. J. F. Airlines at Portsmouth operated Twin Pioneers commercially and Flight One had four of the type for aerial survey work for 20 years from 1972. Only one aircraft remains potentially flyable today, in the hands of Air Antique at Coventry.

Above: *This 1959 Scottish Aviation Twin Pioneer, now re-registered as G-APRS, is owned by Atlantic Air Transport Ltd at Coventry.* ***PRM***

Taylorcraft BC-12/Plus Model C/D

Single-engined, two-seat, high-wing monoplane
Data for Plus Model D
Powerplant: One 48.5kW (65hp) Continental A-65 engine
Span: 10.97m (36ft)
Length: 6.95m (22ft 10in)
Maximum speed: 164km/h (102mph)
First aircraft flown: 1938
Production & survivors: The Taylorcraft Model B and the improved BC-12 was introduced in the USA before the war and returned to production in 1946 as the BC-12D, with more than 2,000 being sold. In the UK Taylorcraft Aeroplanes started to manufacture the Plus Model C in 1938 and continued with the Plus D, which became the Auster I in RAF service. Six Taylorcraft Plus C/Ds are flyable today in the UK and about a dozen imported BC-12Ds.

Above: *This Taylorcraft BC-12D, with wheel spats, is privately owned.* ***PRM***

Above: *Vickers Vimy replica, built in the early 1990s and flown from England to Australia in autumn 1994.* ***PRM***

Below: *The Vimy replica had been re-assembled at Earls Colne early in 1996.* ***DJM***

Vickers FB27 Vimy

Twin-engined heavy bomber

Powerplant: Two 268.4kW (360hp) Rolls-Royce Eagle VIII V-12 water-cooled engines

Span: 20.73m (68ft 0in)

Length: 13.27m (43ft 6.5in)

Maximum speed: 166km/h (103mph)

First aircraft flown: 30 November 1917

Production & survivors: The Vimy was built too late to see war service and it was not until July 1919 that it became fully operational. The 270 built remained in service until the late 1920s when they were replaced by the Virginia. A Vimy flown by Alcock and Brown made the first nonstop Atlantic flight from west to east in June 1919, and Ross and Keith Smith made a record flight from Britain to Australia in the following November. A Vimy replica was built in 1994 and made an anniversary flight to Australia. It returned to the UK in 1995 and remains airworthy.

INDEX